# IDEALIST EPILOGUE

# IDEALIST EPILOGUE

by

## G. R. G. Mure

*Formerly Warden of*
*Merton College, Oxford*

1978

CLARENDON PRESS · OXFORD

*Oxford University Press, Walton Street, Oxford* OX2 6 DP

OXFORD LONDON GLASGOW
NEW YORK TORONTO MELBOURNE WELLINGTON
IBADAN NAIROBI DAR ES SALAAM LUSAKA CAPE TOWN
KUALA LUMPUR SINGAPORE JAKARTA HONG KONG TOKYO
DELHI BOMBAY CALCUTTA MADRAS KARACHI

**British Library Cataloguing in Publication Data**

Mure, Geoffrey Reginald Gilchrist
  Idealist epilogue.
  1. Philosophy
  1. Title
  192      B51      77-30448

ISBN 0 19 824583 1

*Set by Gloucester Typesetting Co Ltd
and Printed in Great Britain by
Richard Clay & Co Ltd, Bungay*

# CONTENTS

# PROLOGUE

I AM not sure that my philosophical career merits an epilogue, but I had an itch to write one, and I thought of composing it in dialogue form, mainly for brevity's sake but also in the hope of imparting a touch of vitality. Yet writers of philosophical dialogue, except Plato, commonly leave one feeling that they would have served their purpose better by straight exposition, or by some sort of Cartesian meditation if they wished to capture benevolence with something a little more human and intimate. I first opened Berkeley when I had been much bored by Locke's *Essay*, and I was eagerly expecting dramatic form to supple the severity of pure thought; but I found that Berkeley had not the art of Plato despite the subtlety of his theme and the beauty of his prose. Hylas and Philonous seemed dreary figures with a tiresome touch about them of the bogus pastoral. Nor, later, did I think that Leibniz gained much by dressing up Locke and himself as Philalethes and Theophilus. Plato, however, not only wrote dialogues but called dialectic the soul's conversation with herself, and I doubt if he came by his more profound conclusions through conversations with his friends and pupils. Epistle VII does not suggest it, and if it had been so Aristotle would have left us a clearer account of the theory of Forms. If dialogue with the pretence of independent speakers was likely to prove frigid, could one talk to oneself? Could one seize and set down without too much artificiality a conversation with that second self whom one talks to and thinks with in philosophical meditation?

I decided to try. At least my *alter ego* need not pretend to an independent personality. I shall evoke him when I put down my pen to reflect on what I have written. He may raise objections, but he will not be merely a *verneinender Geist*. I have no intention of defending my views against all comers. More often he will supplement or elucidate, and on occasion I may allow him a positive idea of his own. In fact he will have no fixed character or function. In all likelihood he will be wildly

Protean, now my conscience, now my caprice, anything from a semblance of the BBC's most offensive inquisitor to a mere alternate voice to break the monotony of exposition. Certainly I shall not claim that our talk is detectably dialectical. I shall try to keep it straightforward, but it may well turn out to be Gonzalo's 'Maze trod, indeed, through forthrights and meanders'; and in that connection I must express my warm gratitude to Professor W. H. Walsh, whose criticisms of my first draft will, I hope, have done something to keep me straight.

I assume to begin with that my other self, in the rare guise of a polite interviewer, has asked me how it was that I took to philosophy, and what beliefs or prejudices survive with me in my old age. My speakers will be labelled 'E' and 'AE', *Ego* and *Alter Ego*.

# I

## INTUITION AND DISCURSUS

. The first question is fairly easy to answer. I went up to Oxford as a competent classical scholar in 1912. By August 1914 I had for rather over a year been reading for 'Greats', the final school of *Literae Humaniores*. It is the best of the Oxford schools, because for four years it keeps the student in immediate touch with the minds of great men rather than with those of mere competent experts. The books he has to read are those which have survived through the centuries as fittest to educate and civilize. Philosophy constitutes half the curriculum. I found it hard and confusing. My tutor, Harold Joachim, struck me as the ablest intellect I had so far met, though I seldom felt that I understood him. By the time war broke out he had, however, imparted to me some sense of the greatness of his subject. That at least, he said, he hoped to achieve as a tutor.

. And that was what attracted you?

. Yes, but I was drawn to philosophy for other reasons, too. I had had no adolescent period of strong religious feeling, and ever since I was confirmed in the Anglican Church at Eton my faith in Christian orthodoxy had half-consciously but steadily declined. I accepted, on the other hand, the general values of western civilization, and I had no doubt of the importance of Christianity in shaping them, and no doubt of the virtues of many good Christians. This was a fairly common attitude in Oxford at the time, especially among idealist philosophers. When I joined the Army in 1914 I should have accepted, if I had yet read them, Bradley's remarks in the Introduction to *Appearance and Reality*: 'Our orthodox theology, on the one side, and our commonplace materialism on the other side . . . vanish like ghosts before the daylight of sceptical inquiry. I do not mean, of course, to condemn wholly either of these beliefs; but

I am sure that either, when taken seriously, is the mutilation of our nature.'

**AE.** You didn't, and you don't, feel that religious myth may meet a specific spiritual need, even if it is quite unacceptable as fact?

**E.** By 'specific' you mean a need distinguishable, if not wholly separable, from the need for moral and aesthetic satisfaction?

**AE.** Yes, and I mean a want and an urge not merely subjective and contingent but as solidly rooted in the nature of things as art and morality; because I suppose that in accepting what you called just now 'the values of western civilization' you would regard moral and aesthetic experience as objectively based?

**E.** I would, but I'm not sure about religion. Is it a species of spiritual value with its own differentia? Or is it, stripped of its sectarian idiocies and cruelties, just the fine flower of morality, Arnold's 'morality touched with emotion'?

**AE.** Stripped of myth, too? I would have thought that in the past most of the good as well as the evil deeds of Christianity had been based on the firm acceptance of myth as fact. Even apart from the lives of the better saints, could a great deal of first-class painting and music have been produced without it? I would have thought, too, that the decay of virtue in the latter half of this century, particularly the virtue of self-control, was at least partly due to the steady diminution of faith in the Apostles' Creed. Something of the same sort may be true of other religions, but I know too little of their history to have an opinion.

**E.** So you would be happy to see God anyhow retained as an invention indispensable to conduct and art? But, seriously, I do admit a great difficulty here, and for the moment I can't contribute to its solution. Let's get on.

**AE.** Well, in 1914 your direct experience of religion was small (and, I take it, still is), but you wanted some sort of rational *Weltanschauung* to justify your more or less Christian values without appeal to myth and miracle, and you thought you might find it in British idealism?

**E.** Yes, and of course I recognized that monotheism, Christian or Spinozistic, was one of the main sources of idealism. But you make it all sound much too clear cut. In August '14 I was philosophically in a very confused and immature state. When war was declared, I was thankful, first, that we were fighting with France and against Germany, and secondly that I should probably not have to sit my final school in 1915.

**ÆE.** And when you came back to Oxford in 1919?

**E.** I came back to Merton wholly undecided about my future. I refused to contemplate any sort of shortened Honour School. Luckily Joachim thought examinations equally detestable from the point of view of the victim and of the examiner. I worked again with him with no explicit end in view. For more than four years I had not read a philosophical book nor even thought much about philosophy, but I found the subject now less baffling and much more exciting. Then Joachim was appointed Wykeham Professor of Logic at New College and, to my very considerable surprise, offered to recommend me to succeed him as philosophy tutor at Merton. So I entered upon the academic life. I doubt whether I should have done so if I had not had four years of war as a regimental officer, but I have never regretted it. I had to work very hard at Greek philosophy and Kant for teaching purposes, and it was twelve years before I published my first book, which was on Aristotle. But I fairly soon began to read Hegel. Wallace's brilliant translation of the *Encyclopaedia Logic* fascinated me. Despite the extreme difficulty of Hegel's texts – how justly did Mme de Staël observe in 1810: 'Les écrivains allemands ne se gênent point avec leurs lecteurs' – the British idealists soon looked to me unduly timid beside him, too concessive, too hesitant in insisting that thought is more than merely adjectival to the singular individual subject.

**ÆE.** Too psychological in their approach?

**E.** Exactly.

**ÆE.** You didn't see Hegel at the root of Prussian militarism?

**E.** I didn't, and he wasn't. Anyhow I thought at that time that I had better read him before I judged him, much as I disliked the Germans and their language. It was after the second world

war that people who obviously hadn't read him – *in primis*
Popper with his notable contribution to ignorance in *The Open
Society and Its Enemies* – began to abuse Hegel hysterically and
blindly.

**AE.** Would you call yourself a Hegelian?

  **E.** Certain Hegelian principles have become immanent in my own
thinking, and when I reflect on them objectively, which I
believe I am still able to do, I can't get away from them. Much
of Hegel baffles me as it baffles everybody else, but I must
count these principles among my convictions, be they prejudices
or not.

**AE.** And just what are these convictions or prejudices?

  **E.** I would prefer to begin trying to answer the question by pro-
posing a view which I first absorbed from Joachim, although it
is certainly Hegelian. It's all in the *Encyclopaedia*, §§61 ff.

**AE.** If I know you – and I ought to – you won't keep off Hegel for
long.

  **E.** I don't intend to. My first conviction I shall put negatively, but
a good deal that is positive follows if it is true. I disbelieve
strongly in the notion of intuition as affording immediate grasp
of a content self-evidently true within, so to say, its own four
corners. I reject such an isolated content of intuition whether it
is offered as rational or sensuous.

**AE.** As you want to proceed negatively, I won't ask you yet for any
positive theory of knowledge. Can we first consider what precise
conception of intuition you are denying?

  **E.** Willingly. Let's get rid of the absurd ones first. Feminine
intuition, if alleged to be not a mere guess but pure of all
inference, is rubbish.

**AE.** But you might perhaps admit that inference can be unconscious,
or only partially conscious?

  **E.** Oh yes. It can easily be forgotten or pass unnoticed. I feel pretty
sure in fact that in some personal relations women are shrewder
than men but less attentive to their own processes of thought.
Next I would exclude prophecy not based on calculation of

chances but claiming direct foresight. Here let me observe how boringly incoherent the script-writers of science fiction become when they try to play tricks with time, slipping their heroes in and out of epochs.

**AE.** Those bogus intuitions gain credence, I suppose, because people find it exciting (and, they hope, profitable) to believe in magical short cuts. But many respectable philosophers have believed in rational intuition as a special way of knowing. I'm not sure about Plato, but certainly Aristotle and Descartes believed in immediately self-evident truths from which dependent truths could be deduced. And Kant believed in sensuous intuition.

**E.** Let's for the moment leave sensuous and concentrate on rational intuition. What you say of Aristotle and Descartes is correct. They were both misled by the analogy of Euclidean geometry, which does start from definitions presupposed and not proved;[1] but the presupposition is only made by virtue of an abstraction from all context. Once the abstraction which founds Euclid's geometry is made, you can perhaps within its limits take the axioms and definitions as purely intuited. On the other hand, the severance of each figure from its context of other figures, and from the properties which complete its nature, is quite artificial. Inference in this field is always hypothetical, and modern mathematicians have long tended to regard mathematical definitions as resting on stipulation. Outside mathematics, and possibly inside it, too, there is, I am sure no pure rational intuition, no truth which does not in some measure depend on a context; very certainly none in philosophy, which does not admit of presuppositions.

**AE.** Which means that there is always an element of inference in the grasp of any limited truth?

**E.** Yes.

**AE.** Aren't you in danger of making any truth so fully determined by other truths that they all have to live by taking in each other's washing? Aristotle insisted on immediate primary and self-evident premises because he saw no alternative but indefinite regress. He rejects solution by mutual laundering, the

[1] In respect of Aristotle see pp. 149–50, below.

view, that is, that propositions can prove each other reciprocally, as leading to mere tautology.[1]

**E.** He is of course quite right in rejecting that sort of circular proof. I'll try to answer your objection, but I shan't be able to without insisting that no human thinking can attain absolute truth, even bits of it. It seems to me that what the pure intuitionists have done, whether in respect of theoretical reasoning or of moral conduct, is to abstract a moment whch is distinguishable but not separable from the inferential or discursive moment of thinking.

**AE.** What exactly do you mean by a 'moment'? I know that idealists borrow it from Hegel to signify something more subtly intimate than 'part', 'element', 'factor', 'aspect' and so forth, but I would like to know exactly what you mean by it.

**E.** The moments of a conceptual whole are distinguishable but inseparable. They could not exist or signify without one another, and each is all-pervasive of the whole. In this case I am convinced that all human experience is both intuitive and discursive, and that it simply could not be either without being the other.

**AE.** So that to regard experience as divisible into discrete patches or sections of each is absurd?

**E.** Precisely. The intuitive moment is the immediate grasp of the experienced content as an indubitably present whole. But there could be no intuition without the moment of mediation, the discursive analysis and synthesis of the whole. Intuition without discursus, so far as one can consider it in abstraction, is the sheerly indeterminate positive.

**AE.** You are saying that the synthesis or, as I suppose it really is, the re-synthesis in the discursus is not by itself the grasping of a whole?

**E.** Indeed it is not. It is the putting together of the analysed elements within the whole which intuition gives.

**AE.** It seems to me that on your account analysis and synthesis

---

[1] See *Post. An.* I, Chapter 3.

should themselves be reckoned two moments of thinking; so that we now have three moments.

Yes I accept that. Three inseparable moments, though of course in a finite individual's thinking psychologically viewed the emphasis will fall now more on one moment, now more on another.

All right, but is not your intuited whole with its analysed and re-synthesized content in danger of becoming logically an isolated monad? Is it not open to the same objection as the alleged intuition self-evidently true within its own four corners? In fact isn't that just what you've now got back to? Yet you did say firmly that every truth was in some measure determined by its context.

Yes I did, and when I said that the intuitive moment was the immediate grasp of the content as an indubitably present whole I left out part of the story. We always in thinking analyse and re-synthesize a whole, and we always determine that whole, however loosely, within a wider whole, an act which belongs to discursus. The whole that we so determine is 'what we are thinking about', the subject of our discourse. This limited whole is certainly not a monad. It is constantly shifting and developing as we proceed, but we confess the presence of a boundary by treating this, that, and the other as relevant to our subject of discourse, but the other, that and this as irrelevant. At the same time we are always aware of our subject of discourse as itself bounded, or perhaps I should say 'selected', within a yet wider contextual whole.

So intuition as such provides an indeterminate whole which discursus limits and articulates?

I think so, but we mustn't try to be too precise. We must try to dissect without murdering, or we shall find ourselves again treating intuition and discursus as separate faculties instead of inseparable moments of thought.

Yes, it's easy to become so deeply absorbed in analysis that you sacrifice the continuous to the discrete and become content to take the synthetic moment, which you can't altogether ignore, as mere aggregation of simples.

**E.** Empiricism Chapter I. It began, I suppose, with the Greek atomists. It didn't attract Aristotle, and the atomists were among his predecessors whom he criticizes in Book A of his *Metaphysics* for not advancing beyond materialism, for speculating on the material causes of things and not their final and formal causes, and very inadequately on their efficient causes. Nor has he much use for the Pythagoreans, who turned all things into numbers. In short, he complains that finding out what things are made of tells you rather little about what they are, and nothing about how or why they came to be so.

**AE.** He was criticizing as a natural *philosopher*?

**E.** Yes. Then Aristotelianism passed away, and natural science followed mathematics in severing itself from philosophy. It was rather like the American declaration of independence, except that happily the U.S.A. did not turn round and try to annex the mother country in the way in which some champions of science and mathematics have tried to inflict their methods on philosophy. Since the divorce, analytical search, aided by mathematics, for the minimal constituents of matter has been the mainspring of advance in physics, especially since the solid Newtonian atom was shattered.

**AE.** Shattered into oddly insubstantial elements. Do scientists really now believe in a cosmos of nothing but electrical charges behaving statistically and not causally, and sometimes at random?

**E.** I wouldn't dare to say, but *qua* scientists why should they not? Science severed from philosophy was bound to envisage its field as value-free and purposeless *in se*. The word 'cosmos' suggests too much of an ordered unity for modern science. Science is theoretical only within narrow limits, but applied to practice its results have, of course, been vast and multifarious. Atomism in philosophy is misplaced, because philosophy is concerned primarily with intrinsic values.

**AE.** In modern philosophy atomism returns, I suppose, with Leibniz. The second paragraph of the *Monadologie* reads, 'There must be simple substances, because there are compounds; for the compound is nothing but a collection or *aggregation* of simples.'

, And the classic British empiricists thought of simple and compound ideas in much the same way. Bertrand Russell took it, I imagine, straight from Leibniz, despite Kant's Second Antinomy.

, How can intelligent men be so naïve? Why should the whole world, mind included, be merely aggregates of atoms?

, It spares one some effort of thinking to believe it. I fancy mathematics has been mainly responsible. When mathematicians with their passion for the certainty of the accurately measurable take to philosophy they inevitably hanker after Pythagoras; but mathematics has always been poison to philosophy.

, Leibniz and Russell were great mathematicians, but Locke and Hume were not. I suppose, though, that mathematics was very much the ideal of certainty in the seventeenth century – even Spinoza felt constrained to geometrize his Ethics – and that is where the trouble began. Already in the mathematical Descartes the discrete is more conspicuous than the continuous. But this seems to give us a good point of transition to the problem of sense intuition.

, Very well. Naturally what I contend against the empiricists, though not of course against Kant, is that an immediately intuited self-evident sense-datum, whether it is alleged to be atomic or to possess internal difference, is just as chimerical as a self-evident object of rational intuition.

, You would say that in any act of sense-perception there must be some sort of discursus?

, In that context I am more in the habit of saying 'interpretation' (though discursus in thought is of course interpretative), but you are right in principle. As you said just now, one must not sacrifice the continuous to the discrete. Singular acts of sense-perception in durationless instants are no more than convenient mathematical fictions. Oh those drearily persistent articles in philosophical quarterlies on Zeno's paradoxes!

, Whether you call it 'discursus' or 'interpretation', what you have introduced into sense-perception looks very like some sort of thinking. You are really saying that any sense-perception is at least rudimentary sense judgement.

**E.** Yes, I accept that. No sensuous content was ever apprehended save through its context and its own internal diversity; and that must be equally true of extra-sensory perception, if there is such a thing.

**AE.** What about the moment of intuition? Does it, taken in abstraction and by itself, provide immediacy and wholeness? How is it going to differ from rational intuition? Aren't you going to turn sense into confused thought, like Leibniz?

**E.** Point taken. I confess to a puzzle not easy of solution. I fancy that Kant, if I understand him, was on the right lines in regarding space and time as not concepts (not 'spatiality' and 'temporality'), but forms of intuition—though of course he has to regard them also as manifolds. They are, I think, wholes or quasi-wholes which we limit in apprehending this or that space, this or that duration. One might call them 'holistic forms'. I would say that in sense-perception we establish, though loosely, a 'this-here-and-now' within a wider spatio-temporal whole, and that the moment of sense-intuition gives (*a*) the indeterminate wider whole, which is limited and ordered by the moment of discurses or interpretation—I don't know what to call it; perhaps 'attention' would be enough at a level of simple sense-awareness—and also (*b*) the direct grasp of the 'this-here-and-now', the sensuous content which attention or interpretation has elicited. I don't much like coining terms, but one might call intuition everywhere the moment of 'holistic immediacy'.

**AE.** And perhaps the discursive moment everywhere 'analytico-synthetic mediation'?

**E.** That'll do. I would adapt Kant by calling intuition without discursus blind, and discursus without intuition empty; but I would regard this contrast as holding, not between thought and sense as such but between the two moments at the levels of both thought and sense, so far as these are distinguishable.

**AE.** When you suggest 'attention' as a name for rudimentary discursus, within what sort of a wider whole does attention select its this-here-and-now? It can't be merely spatio-temporal if only because unfilled space (absolute void) and time save as measuring rest-and-change are only abstractions.

⒉ I would agree, though we perhaps ought to hear what the modern physicist has to say on that subject. I would myself say, following, I think, both Hegel and Bradley, that attention selects within a vague whole of immediate feeling, which is the undifferentiated potentiality of all the sensuous content which we succeed in articulating; and the word 'feeling' reminds me that here are the roots not only of cognitive activity but also of practical and emotional development, from which we have inevitably abstracted in our talk of intuition and discursion. But I don't think we are capable yet of digging deeper into the soil in which these roots grow. Tomorrow I would prefer to turn first to one or two of those Hegelian principles to which I confess attachment if not allegiance.

⒉ All right; but remember that the puzzle of mutual laundering is still unsolved.

# II

## MONISM

**AE.** Today you are to confess Hegelian principles which convince you. I suppose you will eventually discuss the dialectic?

**E.** I don't propose ever to let you tangle me in the detail of Hegel's dialectic, but remember now and hereafter through these talks that its general principle, unsystematized, is simply that what *was* is modified but preserved in what *is*, and that you are accepting that principle if you accept development in any shape. Dialectic is the ubiquitous self-development of spirit, even if one is blind to it or must in certain contexts and for special purposes ignore it. Aristotle saw development in all change, and Hegel tries to expand and systematize—develop, one might say—this principle to articulate an eternal universe. That breeds many problems of detail, but I will start with what offers, I think, as good a way as any to grasping in outline the nature of Hegel's dialectic. That broad stream has many tributaries, and the study of dialectic from Zeno to Fichte, not forgetting Proclus the Neo-Platonist, certainly helped Hegel to shape his method, but it doesn't give us the key. Nor does the polarity of electric and magnetic phenomena.

**AE.** I used to try to find that sort of polarity in every Hegelian triad, but it doesn't work.

**E.** No, and I'll tell you why. It is suggestive but it only prefigures imperfectly the opposites which unite concretely in the true dialectical triad. The poles of the magnet meet in a point of indifference. They do not truly synthesize, because magnetism is only a natural and not an explicitly spiritual phenomenon.[1] The key to Hegel's dialectic lies in Hegel's monism, his conception of an absolute whole. This he more or less took for granted,

---

[1] See *Encyclopaedia*, §24, *Zusatz* 2, para 2; also pp. 164–5, below.

and I confess that I am wholly with him. That all that *is* should in no sense constitute an all-embracing unity is to my mind literally unthinkable. You may in many media *imagine* disconnection, a miscellany of terms standing in no relation to one another. Indeed in practical life and—if that is not a part of practical living—in the pursuit of any special science, you must be prepared to accept disconnections, 'external relations'. In that sphere thinking remains always tied to imagination (or better, 'imaging'), never rises quite clear of it.

**E.** Hegel's *Vorstellung*, 'pictorial thinking'?

**E.** Yes, I accept *Vorstellung* in Hegel's broader sense of the word, and I would like to say a word about the paradox of pictorial thinking, which was really implicit in what we said about sense-judgement yesterday. So far as it is pictorial, so far as it moves in imagery, *Vorstellung* makes no claim to be more than the private experience of a singular finite subject. But when thought makes a sense-judgement out of the content of this imagery, there is at once a claim to objective truth, and truth cannot, like a mere image, be no more than the private possession of a singular finite thinker. A true judgement holds universally, irrespective of this or that particular subject—surely a truism. And yet when a singular thinker claims the content of his judgement as *his* thinking, who shall contradict him? It looks at first sight as if the sentient subject not merely develops in coming to think, but suffers a complete metamorphosis. What wonder if the empiricist shrinks fearfully from the universal and tries to push it under the carpet?

**E.** You mean in fact that the notion of a singular judging subject needs considerable revision? I do indeed fail to see how a strictly singular man can possess a universal thought, philosophical or not.

**E.** Certainly I shall criticize, and with strong conviction, the common notion of a singular experient. In the meantime you will admit that in philosophical thought, however mysterious our possession and exercise of it may be, there is no place for imagery, and consequently no place for pluralism as a philosophical theory? Pluralism is the failure to philosophize; it is ultimately not thinkable.

**AE.** In short, it is the content of a thinking supported, but at the same time hampered and stunted, by imagery which has become irrelevant at a speculative level?

**E.** Exactly, and that means it is error. If you try to think and not imagine pluralism as a philosophical *Weltanschauung* you will be vainly trying to think difference without identity.

**AE.** Again two inseparable moments?

**E.** Certainly. If *per impossibile* you succeeded in thinking sheer difference you would have reduced your universe to dust and absurdity.

**AE.** My *universe* . . . Yes . . . But you and I in our empirical worlds can think impossibles pictorially and hypothetically. How is that possible?

**E.** It certainly is. What would human experience be like if it were not? For the moment I can't frame an answer. May we get back to monism?

**AE.** Hegel, you say, took monism for granted?

**E.** Yes. Apart from the fact that he was the first thinker explicitly to couple identity and difference as inseparable moments, he was a professing Lutheran monotheist, however unorthodox, and the whole tradition of philosophy, pagan or Christian, had been monist. Spinoza, most intensely concentrated of monists, is coupled by Hegel with the Eleatics, and he asserts that every modern philosopher must start as a Spinozist. The long tradition is some evidence of the truth of monism, isn't it?

**AE.** Perhaps. May I now ask what your criterion of truth is?

**E.** Provisionally I would accept Bradley's 'coherence', but that is a notion which needs developing.

**AE.** Would you accept Bradley's kindred doctrine of degrees of truth and reality?

**E.** Yes I would. Incidentally, in expounding that doctrine Bradley confesses himself more than usually indebted to Hegel.[1] Behind both of them lies Plato's teaching in the *Republic* that opining

---

[1] See footnote, *Appearance and Reality*, 2nd edn., p. 318.

contrasts with knowing as dreaming with being awake, and that the objects of opinion are 'between Being and not-being'.

E. I would like to note here, though not for immediate discussion, the onus we lay on ourselves if we accept this doctrine of degrees of truth and reality. As objective idealists, we shall have to show, if we can, that the two sides, the two gradings, are inseparable; that the semi-reality of Plato's shadows and reflections, severed from opinion, has no meaning, though Plato himself simply correlates it with opinion. You will have to bear that in mind when you try to develop the notion of truth as coherence. Meanwhile you would claim only a degree of truth for your convictions?

E. Of course. I fancy I admitted that by implication in denying a severance of intuition from discursion. But let's return to Hegel's monism. He grasped one or two vastly important corollaries. He saw that the universe, all that is, if it had any sort of unity, could be neither finite nor any kind of indefinitely expanding series of terms. So envisaged, it could be no more than a picture-thought, in the latter case indefinitely projected.

E. No more, that is, than its appearance to the man in the street or, with certain qualifications, to the natural scientist. I suppose he learned that from Spinoza and from Kant's exposition in the Antinomies of the contradictions which this kind of series provokes.

E. No doubt. He also saw that a unity of all things, a whole which is absolute at least in the sense that it is not a part of a wider whole, cannot stand in a relation of otherness—as does every finite thing to every other finite thing—to anything beyond itself; for beyond it is nothing.

E. That is fairly obvious.

E. But is it equally obvious to you—pay attention, because this really is the key to Hegel's dialectic—that, since beyond it is nothing, it must be other than itself? Its other, that is, must be contained within it, must in fact be its other *self*?

E. I'm not sure. Why must it have an other, or be other, at all?

E. Because significant otherness is significant negation, and to negate significantly is to determine—what else could give anything a determinate character? If the universe, or for that matter anything in it, altogether lacked otherness it would be a sheer positive, a pure featureless indeterminate. It would have been reduced, if that were possible, to the content of intuition without discursion.

**AE.** Or, I suppose, to sheer identity without difference, to a Parmenidean One. I think I follow that, but it is difficult. I think we should dwell on it and go slow for a bit. When you say *significant* otherness or negation, I take it you mean the assertion of otherness or negation which really signifies in a context of discourse and is not merely true but trivial. For example, 'Intuition is other than (or is not) discursion' would be significant, because the two terms are inseparables which determine one another, whereas Bradley's 'The soul is not a fire-shovel or a ship in full sail' would be true but trivial?

**E.** Yes, and between them the degree of significance in negative judgement can vary enormously. But remember that in a monistic universe even the true but trivial must fall into some sustaining context and possess at least minimal significance. But you would agree, would you not, that if this relative distinction of significant and trivial holds, significant negation is a partial determinant of any finite thing as well as the total determinant of the universe?

**AE.** All right, I'll accept that. We have got back to your allegation of yesterday that every truth is in some measure determined by its context, and my objection about mutual laundering. Can you answer that now?

**E.** I'll try. Following Hegel, I have rejected the vulgar idea of negation as mere erasure, the idea still implied in Kant's primitive notion of the negative judgement as purposing no more than a warding off of error. The complement of that inadequate idea of negation is a cramming of all significance into the positive. The simple positive, whether as an atom or as a self-sufficient singular monad containing internal difference, is then seen as the analytically revealed clue to the aggregates which such simples compose. These aggregates are themselves seen as solely positive, and the relations between their elements are regarded as merely external.

Surely we agreed all that yesterday when we discussed Leibniz and the empiricists in connection with intuition and discursion?

Yes, but I think you have got confused. When I emphasized context and gave negation a much richer meaning as significant determining, you suspected that I was guilty of the converse error: you thought I had erased the positive altogether. By no means. Here again are two logically inseparable moments, not two successive phases of a temporal process. There must be a positive to be determined, but it only emerges under significant determination. It is not something prefabricated, ready-made, *fertig* as Hegel would call it, which stands awaiting determination. To suppose that is to confuse logical with temporal priority. That was the muddle made by the sense-data people like H. H. Price. They argued naïvely that if perception was interpretation there must be an *initial* sense-datum to interpret. The positive, on the other hand, is not a mere prime matter passively stamped with the negations of its neighbours. It emerges to appropriate these determinant negations and constitute itself with some measure of individuality against its neighbours as well as under their determining. With *some* measure of individuality, because the finite things of which we are talking cannot appropriate all the determinations which must in theory go to constitute them. But that is the paradoxical semi-reality of the finite.

Of which we shall doubtless hear more later. I should like to revert to your claim that an absolute whole—or *the* absolute whole, for there could hardly be two—must be other than itself —or must negate or determine itself; for I take it that these have emerged as virtually synonymous. I still don't quite understand.

I said that the absolute whole, if it wasn't to collapse into an utterly indeterminate positivity, must contain its other as its other *self*. I thought I had also made clear that it must, unlike a finite thing, be whole both as itself and equally as its other self.

**AE.** Given an absolute whole, these two conditions do seem to follow.

**E.** Well, prepare for a leap which may seem surprising but is, I am sure, inevitable. Hegel could only meet these two conditions by conceiving his whole as absolute spirit, and as consisting of itself as thinking subject and its other self as existence, or Being as he preferred to call it, following the tradition of Greek philosophy. Thought, on his view, negates and thereby determines itself as Being absolutely. Hence between thought and Being the otherness is absolute opposition: within an absolute whole otherness must be absolute and therefore absolute opposition, not the mere partial difference which holds between finite things.

**AE.** Yes I see; and since that opposition divides the universe, its logical formula will be that of contradiction, A) (not-A. It will not be mere contrariety, which is contradiction confined within a limited system; as, for example, the contraries odd number and even number are contradictories only within the integer series, or as motion and rest are contradictories only within the physical world.

**E.** That is true, but I don't think it is the whole truth. A and not-A in the ordinary logical formula of contradictory opposition divide the universe between them, but only inasmuch as not-A is the mere total absence of A. A and not-A symbolize no significant identity in difference. Thought and Being as thought's other self also divide the universe between them, and so may also be called contradictories. But Being *qua* the absolute negation of thought is not thought's sheer absence. Far from it: through and by virtue of this opposition thought and Being coincide in utter identity. So I think we must say that thought and Being are distinct as well as contradictory, or rather that in this initial opposition and, if I may anticipate, in all the oppositions of Hegel's dialectic, contradiction is fused with distinction in a new form of opposition which is specifically philosophical. That, I think, is the ideal of significant otherness at which Hegel's dialectic aims, though how far it fails in detail and how far the failure was inevitable is another matter.

So that to charge Hegel with violating the law of contradiction is an *ignoratio elenchi*?

Yes, though Hegel might have made clearer what he meant by contradiction. What I have said, which I owe partly to Collingwood's *Philosophical Method*, constitutes, incidentally, a criticism of Croce's separation (is it distinction or opposition?) of distincts and opposites within philosophy. Meanwhile let's reflect for a moment on this initial absolute coincidence of contradictory but *eo ipso* distinct opposites, which Hegel calls the 'original' unity of thought and Being. It may help if we contrast it with (*a*) the realism for which an independent and self-subsistent object-world is somehow copied or reflected in subjective thinking, and (*b*) the subjective idealism which, as I see it, first defines thought against its object without realizing what it's doing, and then denies existence to its object; but subjective idealism is hard to formulate intelligibly.

I presume that in both your Scylla and your Charybdis, so to say, the subject of subjective thinking is any singular finite thinker and no more?

Yes, and I fancy that, conversely, if one takes thinking as no more than adjectival to the singular finite thinker, one is bound to be shattered on Scylla or swallowed by Charybdis, unless one lapses into phenomenalism, which merely leaves one becalmed on the hither side of the dilemma.

But we are not talking, are we, of the singular thinker, but of the self-conscious thinking of absolute spirit?

Quite so. My point here is that on Hegel's view, for which 'objective idealism' is as good a title as any, Being is neither independent of thought nor reduced without residue to thought. The thinking subject, in Hegel's phrase, 'overreaches and grasps', *übergreift*, Being, yet the thinking subject *is*, and what *is* is its other *self*. That is why *Wahrheit*, the ordinary German word for 'truth', has for Hegel the deeper meaning of truth and reality (genuineness) in one. It is at once subjective and objective.

That would seem to be the very paradigm or apotheosis, if philosophy permits the word, of distinguishable but inseparable moments such as we recognized yesterday in intuition and discursus, and today in identity and difference.

**E.** Certainly; and you were right to call the thought of absolute spirit self-conscious. In fact if you will reflect on your common everyday thinking as a finite subject, not your thinking of an external object but your own perhaps rather intermittent and fluctuating self-consciousness, you will get a glimpse of what Hegel means by this 'original' coincidence of opposites. In examining yourself and thereupon condemning or excusing or justifying yourself as thinker or agent; in self-scorn or self-congratulation, self-repression or self-assertion; in a thousand shapes pleasant or painful; you find yourself confronting no mirror image—'Thou turn'st my eyes into my very soul', says Gertrude—but a sharply distinct self with which you yet are patently identical, or else the confrontation could not be. In fact for Hegel, and I find it indisputable, all human thinking is in some degree an overreaching and grasping of its object as an other *self*, always in some measure self-consciousness. It is always in some sense *becoming* its other.

**AE.** And that is the pattern on which you have split me from you and modelled this somewhat contrived conversation? You have raised many questions. You began by maintaining that this Hegelian conception of absolute self-conscious spirit follows necessarily from the notion of monism. An absolute whole must, you said, contain its own negation or otherness as its other self on pain of collapsing into blank positivity—witness, I suppose, Parmenides—but this, you tell me, makes no sense unless the absolute whole is construed as absolute self-conscious spirit. I take it you accept this position yourself, but do you think Hegel reached it by your rather formal and abstract train of reasoning?

**E.** I accept it for at least two reasons. To begin with, there are times when we feel with Wordsworth, 'The heavy and the weary weight/ Of all this unintelligible world'; times when there seems to us to be in all things and all situations an invincible brute particularity, a stupid, opaque uniqueness, devoid of any serious *raison d'être*. We may not have much hope of an answer to our implicit questioning, but unless we are prepared to accept the ultimate unreason of extending this ubiquitous futility to cover the scheme of things entire, we do lessen the oppression of it if we postulate an absolute self-determining whole which could have no *raison d'être* beyond itself to tempt our vain search.

Not wishful thinking?

I don't think so. At least more rational than a pluralism of un-self-transcending miscellanea. Leibniz argues similarly in theistic terms.[1] I might add here that if you once allow the universe as such any *particular* character, you cannot exclude other possible universes without the aid of an external Leibnizian God. In the second place, I think this monistic position is important because it seems to me to hold without dependence on any *special* theistic or spiritual faith. It is quite abstract. Were we to try to give it detailed content we should doubtless soon be in trouble, but as it stands so far I can't get away from it. I am sure, too, that my reasoning is implied in Hegel's system, but he certainly did not arrive at it through no more than what you have justly called a formal and abstract train of reasoning. Hegel succeeded as rightful heir to a very long line of great thinkers, but if we ignore the Greeks for brevity's sake, I would say that, apart from the Protestant religion, the modern foundation of his monism lay in Descartes and Spinoza, with just a hint from Leibniz.

Not Kant?

Oh no. Kant was, I suppose, ultimately a monist, but that does not occur to one as one reads him. He was far too cautious about things-in-themselves, and for that matter about God and reason. Hegel owed plenty to Kant but scarcely monism. In fact for a time the young Hegel was a good deal inhibited by accepting Kant's notion of infinity as indefinite regress, and deducing that reason must remain subordinate to faith.

Your trio, I observe, were all theists.

They were indeed. Hegel's objective idealism is a radical re-construction of theism.

In which God retains an honourable second place, still acknowledged by Hegel, the highly unorthodox but probably quite

[1] *Monadologie*, §§36–41.

honest Lutheran. But let's hear how he appropriates and reconstructs seventeenth-century theistic philosophy.

**E.** It's well worth dwelling on, and I'm not going to hurry. In lecturing on these thinkers he concentrates on what contributes to his own speculation. He tends rather to neglect or depreciate what doesn't, although he borrows from them more than he admits, as I am sure he borrowed his conception of pictorial thinking from Spinoza; but we learn a lot about Hegel. He acclaims Descartes as the hero who reoriented western philosophy on its true course after a thousand years. I don't know what the millenium means, or if it has more than a rhetorical significance. I suppose it might refer to Augustine, who a little anticipated Descartes, but that would mean pushing it back another two centuries. Descartes, says Hegel, achieved his reorientation by starting with thought, and without making any presupposition.

**AE.** How do you do that?

**E.** You set about doubting everything, and you succeed until you find that the existence of yourself as thinking subject is indubitable. The *ego* and its Being are an indissoluble unity which you can't deny without denying yourself, the denier.

**AE.** So here we have the famous *Cogito ergo sum*?

**E.** Yes, and remember that *cogitare* includes all mental activity, even doubting, and that the *ergo* indicates not an inference but the immediate nexus of thinking substance with Being.

**AE.** What does Descartes mean by substance?

**E.** Like Spinoza after him, he defines substance as that which needs nothing else in order to exist. But only God is substantial in the strict sense. The existent *ego cogitans* is an imperfect singular individual, and is substance only in a secondary sense. It is in fact the singular immortal soul of the Christian religion. But Hegel, possibly here taking a hint from Kant's transcendental unity of apperception, transforms this unity of singular thinker and Being, assuming that Descartes, despite his psychological approach, has really revealed the unity of thought and Being as a *universal* nexus.

We touched this morning on the puzzle of how truth could be at once universal and the possession of a singular thinker.

We did, and Hegel's answer is one of those flashes of genius which seems quite obvious when one reads it, although one hadn't thought of it before—or I hadn't. Hegel points out that when a man says 'I' he means himself and nobody else; he thus expresses his individual self-consciousness. But any man can say 'I' with equal right. Willynilly the first man has expressed a universal 'I', the universal subject which differentiates itself in singular thinkers.[1] The universal subject is thus indivisibly one with Universal Being, as the singular thinker, Descartes' *ego cogitans*, is one with the existent self of which he is conscious in self-consciousness.

And the unity of universal subject with universal Being is also a unity of *self*-consciousness. So Hegel gets his 'original' unity of thought and Being, in which Being is the other self of universal thinking subject. I see now what you meant by saying that one's ordinary everyday self-consciousness gives one a glimpse of what Hegel means by his unity of thought and Being, which is 'original', 'primordial', pure of presupposition. Yes . . . when I am attentively self-conscious . . . I *am* aware, without any presupposition or mediation, that I am at once different from and identical with myself. It's really the *Cogito*, Part II.

Quite so, and I find it hard, as I said before, to believe that consciousness of self is totally absent in any human experience. But to continue the story. Descartes's heroic *coup d'essai* bore little fruit within his own system. The *Cogito* did not become a true growing-point. The discrete overbore the continuous. Descartes remained a dualist. Soul and body, thought and extension (to which he reduced Nature), were left as opposed separate entities, created, conserved, and held together only by the supreme but separate entity, God. Then came Spinoza the Jew, who, says Hegel, pushed Cartesianism to its complete logical conclusion. He completely cancelled the separation of these opposites from one another and from God, whose attributes they became. Thus he brought the monism of the East into Europe.

[1] Cf., e.g., *Encyclopaedia*, §20 *ad fin.*

**AE.** In this unity of opposites Hegel, regarding Spinozism as the logical conclusion of Descartes's system, presumably saw a dialectical movement?

**E.** Surely; but although Hegel believed Spinozism to be the essential starting-point of all modern philosophizing, he could not accept as it stood this all-absorbing monotheism. Spinoza's absolute substance Hegel saw as an identity which did no justice to difference. For Spinoza determination is negation, and negation in a nihilistic sense. This really means ultimately that the determinate is illusion. The human understanding and Nature are merely modes respectively of thought and extension. The transition, the logical movement from substance to attribute, and from attribute to mode, is simply ignored. In Descartes everything beyond the *Cogito*, in Spinoza everything beyond absolute substance, is not deduced but merely picked up, presupposed; and in Spinoza's case presupposed only to vanish speedily into the dark abyss of the divine substance. Spinoza was charged with atheism, but he was, says Hegel, not an atheist but rather an acosmist. There was too much God in his system. In their admission of undeduced presuppositions both he and Descartes were seduced by the seeming clarity of mathematics into trying to base their philosophical procedure on the method of Euclidean geometry, which presupposes its axioms and definitions as self-evident.

**AE.** Whereas philosophy, because it concerns the Whole, can allow no presuppositions, as we decided yesterday.

**E.** Quite. I should like to quote you one of Hegel's many penetrating passages about Spinoza: 'The greatness in Spinoza's way of thinking lies in his ability to renounce everything determinate and particular, to address himself only to the One, to be able to heed the One alone. It is a great thought, but it must not be made more than the foundation of all true insight. For Spinoza's One is rigid absence of movement; its only activity is to cast all things into the abyss of substance; all things vanish in it, all life is destroyed. Spinoza himself died of consumption.' And that, Hegel rather brutally suggests, was the appropriate kind of death for him to die.

**AE.** So much for Spinoza; yet he had a point. His *determinatio est* *negatio* does at least warn us that no human thinker, Hegel or anybody else, can show an absolute whole as *absolutely* necessitating any particular feature. What about Leibniz?

, Hegel saw Leibniz's principle of individuality as providing outwardly a way of fusing the fissured Cartesian system with Spinoza's monolith. Not more than outwardly, because although the Leibnizian windowless monads all represent the universe in different degrees of clarity, and although each is an active substance and the concrete unity of its own internal diversity, yet together they form no inter-communicant organic whole but only an aggregate of totally self-enclosed singular individuals.

, As we noted yesterday.

, And the harmony in which they work has been pre-established quite externally——

, By God, the clock-maker, who has wound them all up to keep the right time so far as necessary evils don't clog the works.

, Exactly. We needn't linger over Leibniz, but I think he gives us the right lead-in for a discussion of Hegel's own theory of individuality. That and his theory of negation are to my mind the two greatest triumphs of Hegel's thinking.

, By all means let's discuss that. Carry on.

, Well, I urged that monism implies an absolute which is self-othering, self-negating, or self-determining, and which therefore must be absolute self-conscious spirit. This, I believe, forces one to accept Hegel's doctrine of individuality, which emerges in his Logic as the first of the categories of the Notion (*Begriff*), the first category, that is, of thought as self-conscious. It is in fact his doctrine of the concrete universal.

, We haven't yet discussed the Logic. Could you put that rather more simply?

, Briefly and roughly this is the way I see it. Ordinary people, if they think about it at all, tend to regard the singular individual things which instantiate universals as real and substantial. They can see and touch and hear them, and universals apart from their instances, if they can be brought to entertain the notion at all, seem to them in contrast unreal, *merely* mental and so forth. Empiricist philosophers would agree, and some of them would regard universals as virtually otiose, given good solid particulars. Bertrand Russell at least at one time held that universals might be denied altogether provided that one might still think of particulars as similar. Other philosophers, from Plato onwards, have placed reality in universals on the ground that we think in universals, whereas particulars, singular individuals, are not apprehensible without our very fallible senses unless they are the units of arithmetic, and in neither case are they logically discriminable. Both parties, however, would agree that, if there is universality, it must vary as general and specific.

**AE.** I follow all that—fairly familiar ground. I take it the problem now is, how do universal and particular, general and specific, apply to absolute self-conscious spirit?

  **E.** Yes. If the universe is a single *whole* it cannot be singular, and it cannot be universal in the sense of merely general.

**AE.** Obviously not. If it is whole but not a finite whole among other finite wholes, it must be single and individual without being singular. Am I right?

  **E.** Yes indeed. Let's now start at the other end, so to say. If the absolute whole were completely self-specifying universal, it would be *eo ipso* individual, wouldn't it?

**AE.** Yes it would; and that is the concrete universal, which is emphatically not the singular?

  **E.** Quite so. I said just now that Plato and others placed their faith in universals on the ground that singulars were not apprehensible without the senses unless they were arithmetical units, and in no case are they logically discriminable. I never dare dogmatize about Plato, but he clearly does regard his really real Forms as individuals, although they contrast essentially with the perceptible and semi-real singular individuals which partake of them.

**AE.** Whereas that contrast might tempt one to take the Forms, *qua* universal, as merely general?

Perhaps, but they are norms, standards, criteria, not abstract common characters, not class concepts. The charge of 'reifying concepts' flung at Plato by unperceptive commentators was silly. Plato was feeling after the concrete universal, but he didn't fully realize that to regard the Forms as a plurality is to fail to elevate them fully above the sensible world, and that one Form among many Forms cannot be individual in the sense we are now giving to 'individual'.

Doesn't the Form of the Good in the *Republic* suggest a monistic world of Forms to which it gives Being and intelligibility?

He seldom calls the Good a Form. He says it is 'beyond Being', but I don't think it is the universe as individual. I wonder sometimes whether it may not foreshadow Aristotle's God, but it is only a sketch and we hear no more of it. In the later dialogues Plato struggles with the problem of communion between the Forms, but even in the *Parmenides* he never explicitly asks the question, 'If all that is were One beyond which were nothing, what would be the consequences for the One?'

Besides, the Forms are intelligible but not intelligent. They remain confronted by souls.

So that we can fairly attribute to Hegel the discovery, or at any rate the explication, of the concrete universal.

I take it that if the concrete universal is absolute spirit self-determining from generality through specificity, we have here another pair of distinguishable but inseparable moments?

If it determines itself to individuality, we get more than a pair: we get a complete triad.

And we started this discussion of monism in the hope of finding a key to dialectic.

We did, and the concrete universal *is* a dialectical triad. But before we plunge into the difficult topic of dialectic, remember that we are still at a very early stage. We have tried to show absolute spirit as self-conscious, but we are only just beginning to show it as self-articulating.

Dialectically?

**E.** Yes, but don't hurry me. The archetypal pattern of Hegel's
dialectic is the 'original', 'primordial' if you like, unity of
thought and Being, more precisely the original unity of thinking
spirit with Being. *Qua* original, that unity is immediate, but
thinking spirit alienates Being from itself as at once its absolute
opposite and its other self. That alienation is thought's negation
of itself as Being. But negation, as we saw, is always a significant
determining. Thought's *complete* negation of Being, which Hegel
calls the negation of the negation, or 'second' negation, is not a
frustrated and sterile return to square one, so to say, not a
defeatist acceptance of sheer positivity, but a restoration of the
original unity, not as mere indeterminate positive immediacy
but as concrete re-immediation, positivity enriched by the
negation it now contains.

**AE.** Difficult.

**E.** Yes, but think of the non-transient factor in any process of
development. The difficulty is chiefly due to language. It cannot rise completely clear of imagery; it compels us to use
metaphor and to describe as if it were temporal process what is
not temporal process. The movement of the immediate unity of
thought and Being through determining opposition to concrete
unity is not temporal but logical.

**AE.** That I do see. An absolute whole, spiritual or not, couldn't be
spatio-temporal. If it were it would have an endlessly receding
'other' beyond it. Space and time must be somehow within it.
Change, too; so that it must not only be unextended but, I
suppose, eternal.

**E.** Yes, and if it doesn't change neither can it rest, a point apparently missed by Parmenides. So its eternity cannot be static: it
must be eternal activity.

**AE.** Conversely, I suppose, only activity can be eternal?

**E.** Surely, and when we call this process developing through three
moments 'logical', we have to remember that Hegel's logic is
not formal logic offering validity without guarantee of material
truth. It is committed to his view of the universe. It is ontological. How could it not be, if his dialectic of categories has its

source in the original unity of thought and Being? His logical categories are self-definitions of absolute spirit, of thought in Being and Being in thought. He rejects formal logic, syllogistic logic, except as a sort of elementary natural history of thought, although he attempts a metamorphosis of its forms. He condemns Kant's *a priori* categories inasmuch as they are disconnected and empty till they get sensuous filling, although, again, he adapts them to his own use. He justifies his dialectic as the only true philosophical method on the ground that in dialectic alone are form and content one. Dialectic is in effect for Hegel the outcome, the issue, of the original unity of thought and Being.

. Are you not convicting Hegel of panlogism?

. You mean of making his logic so absolutely ontological that there could be nothing in his philosophical system beyond it?

. Yes, no room for the philosophies of Nature and Spirit.

. I hope not, but I beg leave to postpone that very difficult question. Meanwhile *à propos* of the logicity (I might say 'ontologicity') and non-temporality of the dialectic, take note that the re-immediated concrete unity (the third and consummating moment, that is, of our archetypal pattern and consequently of every succeeding triad in the dialectic) is constantly expressed by Hegel either as the result which contains its own process, or as 'the return upon itself' of the first moment. He expands——

. Half a minute. I'm right, am I not, in thinking that the dialectic, having immanent in it what Hegel calls 'the driving force of negativity', develops in such a way that the triad as a re-immediated unity again divides, begets an opposite self, passes to reconciliation, and so forth?

. Fairly right, but don't get the idea of a rigid formula, and let me get on. Hegel expands his conception of 'return upon itself' to apply to the whole series of dialectical triplicities, or triads, of which his system consists, calling the whole system a circle. That was a simile, but a very important one. This denial of rectilinearity in thought really means that ontological priority and posteriority are relative. Pure thought is neither static nor unidirectional: it moves equally in either direction, which is a clumsy way of saying once again that it is timeless activity.

**AE.** When you say it moves in either direction you presumably mean something different from the vicious circularity we rejected yesterday? I mean the notion of propositions reciprocally proving each other, which only leads to tautology.[1]

**E.** I do mean reciprocity in a sense but not in the sense in which we were thinking of it yesterday. Then we—and for that matter Aristotle, too—were thinking about propositions on the same level, propositions of the understanding Hegel would have said. Dialectic, on the other hand, is the movement of reason and always a development, a lift from level to level.

**AE.** What precisely is the difference?

**E.** I hope it will become clearer when we discuss dialectic *eo nomine*, but I'll do my best here and now to explain what I mean. Hegel starts expounding his logic (or ontologic) with the category of Pure Being. 'Pure' here means simple and indeterminate, not of course pure of thought. He explicitly states that Pure Being *is* pure thought,[2] and that it is the first definition of the Absolute. Every category of the Logic expresses the identity of thought and Being. Hegel justifies his starting point on the ground that Pure Being, since it is so totally featureless that it just collapses into its opposite, viz. Pure Not-Being, is essentially the beginning, because nothing is prior to it, no presupposition attaches to it.

**AE.** So Hegel claims for himself that freedom from initial presuppositions for which he praised Descartes's *Cogito*?

**E.** Yes, but this pure and innocent beginning, although it avoids any empirical presupposition, is far from the whole truth of the matter, as Hegel was well aware. From Pure Being the dialectic develops in the first triad through Not-being to Becoming, which is a mere oscillation of positive and negative in and out of one another, the *eternal* thought of the universe as no more than a universe of all things *endlessly* coming to be and ceasing to be. Thence the dialectic develops through ever more concrete

---

[1] Cf. pp. 7–8, above.　　[2] See *Encyclopae'dia* §86.

categories, the level always lifting. It rises through those categories of Being which succeed Becoming, then through those of Essence and Notion to Absolute Idea, which is the end in the sense of the culmination for the sake of which the process of thought moves, and is the result which contains the whole process in itself. So far so good, but if Absolute Idea is the culmination containing the whole process within itself, it is just as true that the process is the return of pure thought upon itself.

You've got to put together those two ways of looking at it in order to express eternal activity?

That's about it, and here we have the circle symbolizing infinity, not tautology. Moreover, negativity is said by Hegel to be the driving force of the dialectical process. Where, then, does this thrusting negativity come from?

Absolute spirit, I had supposed.

Yes of course, but I mean what is its *proximate* source here? Surely the self-opposition into which Absolute Idea must break because the dialectic is circular.

You are taking the Logic as one circle, although Hegel regards his whole system, Logic, Nature, Spirit, as a circle?

Yes I am. Every triad is a circle, a return of the beginning on itself. In the *Science of Logic* Hegel says clearly that logic is a circle in which the first is last and the last first.[1] Doubtless Pure Being is sheerly positive, blankly indeterminate, *vis à vis* what follows, but it is, within logic, the utter opposite, the absolutely negated self, of Absolute Idea. If the Logic is a circle, Absolute Idea must have an opposite *within logic*. What except Pure Being could fill the bill? The force of negation drives on the thought of Pure Being, more and more fully determining it, until it develops into Absolute Idea. This negation, on the other hand, could not operate unless Absolute Idea were, so to speak, drawing back into itself the other self which it alienated in the initial shape of Pure Being.

[1] Cp. Hegel's Works, Jubilee Edition, Vol. 4, pp. 74–6, and Miller's Translation. pp. 71–2.

**AE.** So Absolute Idea is, as it were, at once the final and the efficient cause of the ontological development?

**E.** I take it you refer to Aristotle's conception of specific form as both efficient and final cause of maturation in the specimen. A good analogy, and one might helpfully add Aristotle's doctrine that if you complete temporal process so that it fully contains its own end at any and every instant of itself, it then becomes not static but a timeless activity. Indeed I can't think of a better way of expressing true activity.

**AE.** Good. Are you now prepared to defend Hegel against the charge of panlogism?

**E.** No; that problem takes a lot of thinking about. I will try to tackle it, but not yet. For the moment I'm tired. We have dwelt too long in a rare and exhausting atmosphere. Tomorrow I propose to start with a confession of ignorance, but I shall try to justify it.

# III

## KNOWLEDGE AND IGNORANCE

**C.** Today you are to confess your shortcomings?

**L.** Yes, and my first confession is this. Yesterday I offered as my own conviction a very bare outline of the principles of Hegelian idealism. But what right had I to that conviction?

**C.** You said when I asked you that you would provisionally accept coherence as your criterion of truth. Bradley reasonably added comprehensiveness to coherence as his criterion. Were you not convinced of your spiritual monism because you judged it more coherent than other philosophies, and more comprehensive because it included them or some of them?

**L.** Perhaps I was, but there seems to me to be something missing in the bare statement of truth as coherence and comprehensiveness.

**C.** What's the matter with it?

**L.** Can you tell me how to differentiate coherence from mere consistency? Error can be internally consistent.

**C.** I'm not sure I want to differentiate them if comprehensiveness is added to coherence. I thought that in any theoretical field one theory usually superseded another because it was wider and more consistent than its predecessor, and that that was the progress of truth.

**L.** That's all right so far as it goes, but how do we know that this alleged 'progress of truth' is more than the wider error succeeding the narrower?

**C.** Can error have no degree of truth in it?

**L.** Possibly not, but that is not the point. If you take the criterion of truth as simply consistency plus comprehensiveness, you make thinking purely subjective and hypothetical. The difference between truth and error vanishes, and you have to turn realist and change your criterion of truth to correspondence with an independent object, a wholly unverifiable relation which, if accepted outside everyday thinking, leads to a philosophically unthinkable pluralism. I distinguished coherence from consistency because I thought that there was something more than consistency in Bradley's coherence. If we accept, as I do, Hegel's conception of truth as the unity of truth in the vulgar sense with Being or reality and make coherence the criterion of it, then coherence must be objective and categorical, not subjective and hypothetical and so divorced from Being. Consistency to become coherence must be underpinned by Being.

**AE.** All right. Proceed with your confession.

**E.** I will, but once again don't hurry me. We have learnt, or should have learnt, from Descartes to worry now and again about the authenticity of our own thinking. When I do this I find myself on the horns of a dilemma which has gored other people besides me. On the one hand, in any field of experience I am bound in the end to trust my own judgement. If I accept someone else's, I do so because I *judge* that he knows better than I. I can no more deny intellectual responsibility than I can deny moral responsibility.

**AE.** When the question is theoretical, you can refuse to decide, can't you?

**E.** Perfect Pyrrhonism, complete refusal to decide, isn't thinking. The totally open mind is chimerical, though one meets irritating approximations to it. Thinking is judging, and judgement can never be totally suspended. That was one of Descartes's errors. I deny, with the later Bradley, the entirely free-floating idea. Any idea is attached in some world, and there is at least an implicit judgement affirming or denying it there. That follows equally from Hegel's conception of *Wahrheit* as fusing truth and reality.

**AE.** What about illusion, hallucination, dream, madness? In all of these there is at least a simulation of judgement. Will you say that the content affirmed in all of them has a place in a real world, however low its degree of reality?

**E.** Indeed I would. Just now you suggested, rather irrelevantly, that error must have some degree of truth in it. In fact I agree with you, and all the phenomena you speak of are types of error. The ordinary man would contrast them as purely subjective and unreal with the world of his daily life, which he calls 'real' mainly because he assumes its objects to exist independently of himself, perhaps also because they sometimes hurt him. In daily life the contrast serves well enough for practical purposes. We try to escape illusion, we shut up madmen, and most of us attach small importance to our dreams. Yet these errors draw their content from the 'real' world of daily life, the world of 'actual fact', and however much they disintegrate and pervert it, they still possess the rags and tatters of its reality.

**E.** You would add, I suppose—I think you must if your position is to stand up—that this 'real' world of daily life, the world of mainly pictorial thinking, has itself no very high degree of reality if we apply the standard of coherence; more importantly, you would say that, although in daily life we experience a largely common world, a 'public' world, that is no ground for supposing it a world independent of experience. If, then, this crude realism won't do, and we are never totally severed from objective Being, no experience, even that of the madman and the dreamer, can be totally subjective.

**E.** True. What 'real life' is is the million dollar question, but total unreality is a myth. Now let me get back to my dilemma. I said I was bound always to accept intellectual responsibility and trust my own judgement. The other horn of it is this. Even when I am only trying to formulate a problem, I find, if I reflect, that I have already committed myself to many assumptions which I couldn't justify if challenged, although I am convinced that at least some of them are true.

**E.** The situation Hegel tried to avoid by starting his Logic with Pure Being?

**E.** Yes, but that doesn't mean he started with his mind a *tabula rasa*. He admitted that a thinker cannot jump out of his own epoch. Anyhow I'm not nearly as tough and confident as Hegel. I suffer from an intellectual guilty conscience before I've written a page on any philosophical subject. I have a sense of cheating, too, when I use a metaphor or a simile, although I can't avoid them, because that is the way language has developed. All these things burden my mind like (forgive the simile) an overdraft at the bank. I know that I cannot live within my means and must borrow. At the same time I am puzzled by the undeniable fact that I am self-critical, that my thinking has in it an immanent criterion which makes me aware of my indebtedness and the insecurity of my intellectual resources.

**AE.** Can you solve this dilemma? Can you show these opposites (if they are opposites) passing into a unity?

**E.** I doubt if that is quite what the situation demands. Let's try to take our bearings. We have outlined our spiritual monism, and I have told you that I do not intend to get lost in the detail of the dialectic: I can only suggest how it ought to be approached. But I think we might do something to fill in our outline by trying to consider human beings as constituents of absolute spirit. That might in the long term help us to solve my puzzle.

**AE.** Consider them as elements of that other self which moves towards reconciliation?

**E.** Yes.

**AE.** In that case absolute spirit and a human being will be in some sense mutually constituent?

**E.** Mutually *self*-constituent, I would say.

**AE.** Very well, but that will commit us to two more Hegelian doctrines, I think, though we are already pretty well committed to the first.

**E.** Go ahead.

**AE.** The first is negative, though doubtless also determinant: Hegel's contention, I mean, that the world of man and Nature is neither a pantheistic emanation from absolute spirit in which all things are indiscriminately divine, nor a world in one-way dependence on Aristotle's remote and unaware God to whom it strives to assimilate itself. Both these views are ruled out by his conception of the world as absolute spirit's other *self*.

**E.** A conception which Hegel rather effectively reinforces in the imaginative terms of religious myth when he says that the Logic may be regarded as the content of God's mind before the Creation, and that the Creation is no arbitrary act of God but his necessary self-fulfilment, a free but inevitable self-determination, lacking which God would not *be*. And God, he thinks, must manifest himself without reserve: Christianity is *par excellence* the revealed religion. In the Philosophy of History lectures Hegel says, *Nichts ist wesentlich, was nicht erscheint*: 'Nothing has essential being which does not appear.'[1] This follows from the self-consciousness of absolute spirit. Every category of Essence, the middle section of a Hegel's Logic, is the thought of at once a coupling and a conflict of an essence with its appearance. Hegel often insists on this necessity of self-manifestation. One reason for its importance is that it is a denial of realism: what must manifest itself cannot subsist in independence of all consciousness.

**E.** To most of that we were already committed. But there is another important, indeed indispensable, doctrine of Hegel which you are going to need, namely what he calls the 'ideality of the finite', and regards as the chief maxim of philosophy and the real reason why philosophy must be idealist.

**E.** Oh certainly, and we had better be clear what it is. Hegel holds that the being, in the sense of the full nature, of any finite thing lies always beyond it.

**E.** Whereas absolute spirit has no context. Beyond it is nothing, so that in this relation it may be called infinite?

**E.** Yes. A finite thing is determined by a context which recedes from it *ad indefinitum*.

**E.** A less misleading expression for endless regress than *ad infinitum*?

**E.** I think so. It is Hegel's *schlecht unendliches*, the bad or spurious infinite, which is only the repetitious negating or othering of the singular. That endless recession doesn't much matter to us in practical everyday life, because there only certain features of the finite thing concern us. It is for us, for our apprehension, sufficiently individual to let us recognize and use it, be it the refrigerator, the gas-cooker, or the washing-machine. That is

[1] See also *Encyclopaedia*, §131.

enough for us. But if we are perseveringly curious and ask persistently what is it, we shall find ourselves predicating qualities and relations of it indefinitely and still failing to grasp it as unique. We may try to distinguish its essential from its accidental characters, but even so any definition we reach will be a compromise.

**AE.** You are at present talking only of finite things which are either inanimate or at any rate below the level of self-consciousness; things of which Hegel would say that their *an sich*, what they are in themselves, is not *für sich*, not for them an object of which they are conscious, but only *für uns*, only an object for our consciousness?

**E.** Yes; I'll get on to human beings in a minute.

**AE.** This time let me ask you not to hurry. I should like to do a little meander, which may only lead us up a *cul de sac*, but I'm not sure. I've always been intrigued by this fairly frequent phraseology of Hegel. Does he only mean that the mountain and the gas-cooker, the cabbage and the cat (always assuming that she isn't self-conscious, which I rather doubt) don't know what they are, but we do? That seems to me rather too easy. After all, the whole non-self-conscious world, everything that the special sciences investigate from mathematical entities to subhuman mammals, and even human mammals so far as they are below the explicitly self-conscious level—all that world is in Hegel's view an element in absolute spirit's self-conscious dialectic. Could he mean that this world, whose *an sich* is only *für uns*, has Being by virtue of Absolute Spirit's knowing it (as an element of its other self) *through our knowing it*?

**E.** Always of course remembering that only what is known *is*. But I'm doubtful of your suggestion. Certainly the non-self-conscious world has Being by virtue of the unity of thought and Being. Therefore it does not exist in self-sufficient independence. But neither does it exist like Alice imagined as no more than a creature in the Red King's dream, if only because a great deal of it existed before the human race existed, and will pretty certainly go on existing after man's extinction. Why, then, should absolute spirit know it only through our very incomplete and transient knowledge of it?

, I didn't say *only* through our knowing. My answer would be that our knowing goes to constitute absolute knowing, and a part of what it contributes must be our very defective and, if you like, transient view of the non-self-conscious world.

, In other words every constituent organ of the Absolute is an only partly true and real approximation to itself?

, At any rate for us it is, and that on your account must be all that we ourselves can be for ourselves.

, Well, I have accepted degrees of truth and reality. But this is getting very difficult. Would you agree to a verdict of 'not proven', or at least remand the case till we have discussed the ideality of a human being?

, That's what we really want to get at, so I agree.

, Since a finite human being is *für sich* as well as *an sich*, I suppose we must say that his ideality is his whole *nisus in esse suo*, physical and mental; his aspiration never fully to be satisfied, to realize himself as an element of absolute spirit in whom absolute spirit constitutes itself; in short, his *nisus*, conscious in *very* varying degrees of its ultimate end and aim, thrusts and strives in every human pursuit, in love and war, in learning and art, in——

, Spare the rhetoric. At the moment we are only concerned with the philosopher pursuing truth.

, Very well. I promised for today a confession of ignorance and an attempt to justify it. Man's aspiration to know is partly achieved, because absolute spirit thinks in and as man, but its complete achievement would *per impossibile* destroy the difference between absolute spirit and its finite constituent, upon which the whole theory rests. Therefore the finite thinker must be at once knowledgeable and ignorant, knowledgeable by virtue of the immanence, the self-constitution, of the Absolute in him, ignorant because he is only one constituent and constituted element. His knowledge of spirit immanent in him is defective, a loan which he must accept because he cannot fully justify a claim to be drawing only on his own funds; but this knowledge cannot be illusory, because it constitutes him—

remove it and he *is* not. Moreover, it carries with it self-criticism: awareness of his own ignorance is a necessary factor of his knowledge.

**AE.** And that is how you excuse your ignorance. Very well, provided you don't take a too easy way out into agnosticism. All the same, I don't altogether grasp your position here. So far as I think I do understand it, it seems to me to be equally hard to defend or attack. I found your outline sketch of a monistic spiritual universe almost as convincing as you did. You owed most of it to Hegel, but it was bare enough to be moderately undenominational. From the logically incontestable necessity that a monistic universe must contain its own other you deduced that such a universe must be a dialectic of self-conscious spirit, a timeless 'circular' self-development of spirit as the unity of thought and Being. So far this outline has remained pretty featureless. We have not yet seen how the dialectic in virtue of its origin must work. So far, however, I was fairly well satisfied. But today, in asking yourself what right had you to your conviction of spiritual monism, you brought the finite and the infinite into contact in a way that confuses me.

**E.** Is 'contact' quite the right word?

**AE.** Perhaps not, but that is where I begin to lose my footing. You talk about absolute spirit and a human being as being mutually self-constituent——

**E.** You seemed to accept that when I said it.

**AE.** Yes, and I seem to remember Hegel getting very obscure in his attempt to express that sort of reciprocity of two self-consciousnesses; but on reflection I can't make sense of it. I suspect that you are trying to talk from two points of view, from two different levels, at the same time. I can think of two human beings as in part mutually constituent, even mutually self-constituent. I think of perfect lovers, the Phoenix and the Turtle; of partnered dancers, Nijinsky and Karsavina; of Isaye and Pugno playing Beethoven violin sonatas; even of close co-operants in 'enterprises of great pith and moment'; I don't even forget that in the highest form of friendship, according to the sober Aristotle, each friend is the other's other self. All these pairs no doubt in some sense create themselves in each other, but they meet on the same level of Being and are united for a limited period of time.

. Always on the same level? Are the composer and the executant on the same level? And is time of much importance here? When Isaye and Pugno played his sonatas, Beethoven was long dead, but when they played surely he inspired them, a word which means nothing unless it means he became a constituent of them? Surely their performance and those of thousands of nineteenth- and twentieth-century singers, instrumentalists, and conductors—to say nothing of composers who learned from his music—have entered into the being of Beethoven and Beethoven into theirs? Or take the stage. It has been opined that Salvini's performance of *Othello* was the greatest ever. Was there no reciprocal constituting of actor and author, even if Shakespeare wasn't sitting in the stage box? And what was the situation when Boito and Verdi created on Shakespearian texts one, if not two, of the greatest operas ever written? One need not put faith in the survival beyond death of singular individual souls in order to believe that a man's stature may grow beyond the grave. Hegel very justly proclaims that a man's reality lies, not in his *an sich*, not in what he is merely in himself and implicitly, but in what he achieves. Where is the limit to that? The effect of his actions, his paternity, for I suppose the continuity of the germ-plasm counts for something, whatever the shape it grows into; the inspiration of his art and thought on later generations, which counts for much more—in all that tide of him which flows on unchecked by the passing bell, a great man grows and his reality extends. By that most true standard we may say without appeal to a miraculous resurrection that Jesus of Nazareth grew stupendously. There is nothing in the least unreal or metaphorical about the immortality of Homer, Phidias, Pericles, and Plato; of Julius Caesar and Virgil, Dante, Shakespeare, and Michelangelo. *Pulvis et umbra sumus*, no doubt, yet the same poet's *non omnis moriar* was not an idle boast. Can we really believe that, failing an ascent of singular souls to Heaven, death flatly annihilates the men who have given us the life-blood of our minds? If the human race perished, this reality would not wholly perish with it, because it has a timeless dimension, and the timeless is not the everlasting but the eternal. Nothing is more finite than death. Don't attach too much importance to it. When it comes near, just hope you may have contributed something.

**AE.** I'll try. You'll be there to help. Meanwhile I point out that you still haven't raised the source of inspiration-cum-feedback—if I may react a shade frivolously to your rather funereal last remark—higher than the still prima facie finite human being, the great man in any field. But on your showing finite man, great or small, has got to be inspired and constituted *in toto* within an Absolute beyond which is nothing.

**E.** Certainly, but absolute spirit is not a transcendent God over and above the approximations which constitute it. Finite man can at best know the Absolute only as he finds it in and as man, as the presupposition of his own spatio-temporal finitude and the timeless fountain of his values.

**AE.** What he finds in him of infinity he knows, you would say, rather than guesses or wishfully thinks?

**E.** Yes, because it *is* himself, as I said before.

**AE.** But surely he can ignore it or at least misconstrue and pervert it?

**E.** He can, because, as we agreed just now, a dialectically self-severing and self-reconciling absolute spirit can only constitute itself in partially true and real approximations to itself. I will add here—and it is vitally important—that his knowledge and his ignorance will not be mutually exclusive. At any rate in his thinking so far as it is rational, pure and not pictorial, knowledge and ignorance will overlap. His learning is never sheer novel increment, but always a coming to know better what he knew less well before. That is why his ignorance is never absolute and why he could not err if he had not truth to pervert. Purely subjective thinking, as I thought we had made clear, is chimerical. This overlap of knowledge and ignorance finds confirmation, too, in our doctrine of the inseparability of intuition and discursus, our disbelief in fragments of absolute incorrigible truth.

. If finite man, as you agreed, has got to be constituted *in toto* within the Absolute, you must surely admit that even within pictorial thinking, and in the depersonalized and aseptic version of it in which I suppose natural science consists, and again even in mathematical manipulatory thinking, the subject does come to know better what he has known less well, and that even his knowledge and ignorance do in some measure overlap?

. Yes, but to a far lower degree, and those are not the distinctive characteristics of that sort of thinking. To the subject who thinks in any of the fields you speak of his object necessarily appears to be independent of his thinking about it. If you questioned him, he would probably tell you that he didn't see how, unless it were independent of his and everybody else's thinking, there could be any truth about it. He would tend, unless some old fashioned philosopher had got at him, to regard any advance in his knowledge as new increment rather than as a better knowing of what he knew before, because he would not be thinking of himself as inspired, but rather as confronting an object-world to be explored as his sole possible source of information. He would confess to some doubts, but with a special scientist's liking for exact measurements and definite classifications, he would prefer to maintain, so far as he could, hard-edged areas of knowledge, ignorance, and doubt. I call his attitude necessary because, if he didn't make these mainly unconscious assumptions, he would not achieve the kind of result which he aims at as an ordinary practical man or as a special scientist. Being unconcerned with values, he must be as faithful as he can to facts.

. But if he didn't make these assumptions and knew better what truth is, wouldn't he be a better scientist?

. No. You seem to forget that we have accepted degrees of truth *and reality*, degrees of *Wahrheit* we might now say. We have also confessed that absolute spirit must, paradoxical as you may still find it, constitute itself of approximations to itself, just because it is at once the source and the consummation of the 'circular' dialectic in which it consists. If then, as I suppose, ordinary thinking and special science approximate to absolute spirit only in a degree, their relative lack of *Wahrheit an sich* (apart, i.e., from their ultimate nature within the Absolute) must be a defect equally in subject and object. The world which the finite thinker at this level knows can't be a fully real world, and he himself cannot be fully real; but his finite purposes are not for that reason less well served.

**AE.** That recalls opinion and the semi-real in Plato's *Republic*.[1] Anyhow you think he's all right so long as he doesn't try to philosophize with scientific methods or common sense. Aren't you being a shade arrogant? Even your outline of spiritual monism—indeed even your undenominational monism before you deduced its spirituality—can only be knowledge pervasively tinged with ignorance. You have called your Absolute the time-less fountain of man's values (echoing Bernard Bosanquet, I think), and that compels you to affirm it as self-constituent in the inspiration of man's thinking, his conduct, his art, and of any other human value which you may regard as intrinsic. You might try, as Hegel tried, to articulate absolute spirit as the eternal activity which manifests itself—exhaustively, so far as you are able to tell—in all the struggles of man to transcend himself, in all the ideality of the human finite. If beyond the Absolute is nothing, you would have to include, as Hegel in-cluded, Nature on earth organic and inanimate, and indeed the whole cosmos. But in all your speculation your knowledge and your ignorance would never cease to overlap.

**E.** Certainly. That is what I set out to confess. I don't see why you should call my attitude to science arrogant. I criticicize not science but scientism. If the misuse of science sometimes makes one think that it might have been better to follow the example of Butler's Erewhonians and prohibit it some time ago, that is not the fault of science but of the use men make of its dis-coveries. It might be argued that the aid of science in the devel-opment of medicine does not compensate for the horrors made possible by splitting the atom, but to attach moral blame or credit in the perfectly neutral and value-free field of science is absurd.

**AE.** I didn't suppose you wanted to abolish science, but you seem to think that, except for practical purposes in which science is

[1] Cf. pp. 16–7, above.

needed as a means and not as an end, philosophical knowledge-and-ignorance which overlap are somehow superior to scientific or mathematical knowledge and ignorance which do not overlap, or do so to a lesser extent.

. I only meant that you can't apply the scientist's and the mathematician's notion of knowledge and ignorance in philosophy. There is a difference of kind and . . . well, yes, also a difference of degree. But comparisons are odious.

. Yet surely inevitable in honest philosophizing. What you say seems to me to clamour for discussion. Please expand.

.. The philosopher's primary function is to make what sense he can of spirit. All else he must treat as ancillary. Philosophy is therefore concerned primarily with the real in its aspect or moment of intrinsic value, and with fact in so far as it embodies value, or stands in some significant relation to intrinsic value, be it contrast or prefiguration. If the fountain of values is absolute spirit of which we are organic particles, our philosophical experience is bound to be a blend of knowledge with ignorance (and consequently error) such that it would be equally ridiculous either to suggest an exact ratio between the two elements or to hope for the total conquest of ignorance in either the whole field of our philosophizing or in any corner of it.

.. I take it that you are about to contrast dialectical reason with the thought of the 'understanding', Hegel's *Verstand*, as expressed in neutral, value-free science and mathematics, which aim single-mindedly at precise exactitude. Don't you risk turning philosophy into faith? Hegel spent a lot of effort trying to do just the opposite.

.. I don't think so. Understanding is sublated in reason, as Hegel makes very clear in the Logic, and reason is therefore determinate but not rigid. You'll see the difference if you contrast rigid *a tergo* causal determination with self-determining freedom, for which the scientific understanding has no place. But freedom has causality in it: it would otherwise be mere caprice, sheer contingent liberty of choice.

.. That is a very helpful illustration of sublation. Does understanding differ from reason as consciousness from self-consciousness?

**E.** I would say that all thought is self-critical and to that extent self-conscious. The scientist is formally aware that he is thinking, and of course criticizes with his own criteria the conclusions of his scarcely personal thinking about an object which he regards as wholly independent of himself. But philosophical thought is not only self-critical. Absolute spirit is immanent in it, and intrinsic value, as I hope to show you more clearly later on,[1] is a most vital moment in the reality (*Wahrheit*) of absolute spirit. Hence philosophical thought is at once conscious of itself and of value.

**AE.** You imply that scientific and mathematical thought is not in any developed and concrete sense self-conscious, because its value-free object is independent of it, and it does not in free dialectical movement reflect and explicate the activity of a universe in which reality and value are one? That is why for the scientist, and even more for the pure mathematician, knowledge and ignorance tend to fall apart. Their *ignorantia* is not *docta*.

**E.** That is why they find it so hateful. They have a desperate longing for absolute certainty. This is no doubt less true of the biologist in his more concrete field, but in general faithfulness to fact tends with them to become a moral principle almost fanatically held; and this ethical aspect is hard to explain if, like Bertrand Russell, they divorce value from thought and assign it to feeling alone.

**AE.** You mean that if, as the emotivists hold, intrinsic value can only be felt and not logically defended or attacked, it is hard to see how knowledge of a value-free world can itself have a value to which a scientist or a mathematician *ought* to be loyal?

**E.** Yes. The contradiction into which emotivism is forced springs from a mistaking of understanding for reason. But to return to this craving for certainty. The first aim of Russell and other symbolic logicians was to guarantee the certainty of mathematics, and when Russell claimed to have identified mathematics and logic, he believed that he and Whitehead had gone far towards doing so. When knowledge-and-ignorance turned up in the clean clear logico-mathematical world in a rather overlapping sort of way, it drove Russell and Frege nearly frantic.[2]

[1] See p. 105, below.
[2] See R. W. Clark, *The Life of Bertrand Russell*, Weidenfeld, 1975, pp. 80–2.

**.** What caused the trouble?

**.** It was a paradox like the statement of the Cretan Epimenides that all Cretans were liars. Russell one day reasoned (if I've got it right) like this: 'The class of all classes is a class, but there are classes which are not members of themselves. If these latter form a class, is that class a member of itself?' The puzzle was eventually solved, but at the time it was thought to ruin any hope of establishing the foundations of arithmetic. When Russell, in the name of philosophy, tried to fit other fields of Being to this intensely rarefied logico-mathematical form, the result, at least at one period of his speculation, was neutral monism. His theory was that the atomically simple, which you must aim to reach by analysis, is in principle the indubitably certain and is the clue to the complex, which accordingly, since all relations are external, is an aggregate.

**.** As we decided in our first talk.

**.** Analysis of experience should produce, so Russell held, particulars as nearly atomic and indubitable as it is possible to dig down to. With these bricks aggregated in series (there thinks the mathmatician) you should be able to build up logically both the entities commonly called mental and those usually assigned to matter. For these atomic bricks are fashioned out of a neutral stuff—Russell, you will observe, seeks the indubitable not in the *ego* but in the neutral atom—and they are, more nearly defined, dual-natured evanescent events. In one aspect and situation the event is a sensation, and so 'mental'; in the other it is physical. With these and more dubitable elements, namely *sensibilia*, which *qua* unsensed are physical, and images which are purely psychical, a unified mind–matter world is to be constructed. In one aspect it will obey the laws of psychology, in the other the laws of physics, but as philosophy matures towards science the laws of physics will more and more predominate. Nevertheless Russell does confess that he may not have succeeded in escaping solipsism. This is the bare gist of Russell's *Analysis of Mind* so far as I understand it.[1] C. D. Broad remarked justly, 'Mr. Russell produces a different system of philosophy every few years', but Russell was fifty when he published this work. It does not lack

[1] I dealt with the book at more length in *Retreat from Truth*, Blackwell, 1958, Chs. V and VI.

ingenuity, but what a wretchedly narrow and poverty-stricken piece of speculation!

**AE.** It was an offering on the altar of that faith in truth as mere exactitude which you called fanatical. What more could you expect from a man with that logico-mathematical past? His determination to subject philosophy to the exactitude of mathematics and science reminds me of Voltaire's remark so well expressing the misconceived ideal which fettered and contracted French poetry in the seventeenth and eighteenth centuries: 'Les vers, pour être bons, doivent avoir l'exactitude de la prose, en s'élevant au dessus d'elle'. Good poetry has its own discipline, which is not enshrined in Malherbe and "the rules". So has good philosophy, but it *sublates* the understanding. It does not retain its rigour unchanged.

**E.** Whereas, you mean, the French poetry of that period retained so much exactitude that it doesn't rise very far above prose?

**AE.** Yes, its wings have been too closely clipped. But to return to Russell. When he first brought his scientific convictions into his own philosophizing, by which I mean his own self-conscious experience of value, they brought him no joy. *A Free Man's Worship* is a a moving expression of mental agony. Twenty-five years later *Why I am not a Christian* registered no change: 'Fundamentally, my view of man's place in the cosmos remains unchanged. I still believe that the major processes of the universe proceed according to the laws of physics.'

**E.** And he never asks himself whether, if that were the whole story, the laws of physics co-operating with the lawlessness of contingency, could have produced the human beings who constructed them; surely a deadlier dilemma than the puzzle about classes.

**AE.** His *Weltanschauung* is very much a naïve throwback to the Epicureanism of Lucretius, but Lucretius felt much more cheerful about man's very finite destiny than did Russell.

**E.** What saddens me is that it was all so unnecessary. Russell was a man of genius; he wrote a classically beautiful English prose unexcelled by any other author of his time; he was full of immortal longings, forbidden to flower into philosophy by a misplaced predilection for exactitude, and a monstrous banishment of value from thought. Oh the pity of it! What do you make of this to Ottoline Morrell? 'I think I have always felt that there were two levels, one that of science and common sense, and another, terrifying, subterranean and periodic, which in some sense held more truth than the everyday view. You might describe this as a Satanic mysticism. I have never been convinced of its truth, but in moments of intense emotion it overwhelms me. It is capable of being defended on the most pure intellectual grounds—for example, by Eddington's contention that the laws of physics only *seem* to be true because of the things we choose to notice.'[1]

I fancy Russell did eventually begin to lose some of his optimism about certainty, largely under the influence of that terrible purist of the same sect, Wittgenstein. Your quotation does sound like a broadening outlook—it's surely not neutral monism—but why 'subterranean' and 'Satanic'? Did it seem a Devilish assault on the sanctity of science? What about this, also to the Egeria who did so much to humanize him? 'I want to bring back into the world of men some little bit of new wisdom. There is a little wisdom in the world; Heraclitus, Spinoza, and a saying here and there. I want to add to it, even if only ever so little.'[2]

A more philosophic urge perhaps, though a somewhat grudging recognition of extant human wisdom. Whitehead was much more truly a philosopher.

Yes indeed, and who more suitable than Whitehead to supply the antidote to Russell? Let me read you this from *Process and Reality*:[3] 'Philosophy has been haunted by the unfortunate notion that its method is dogmatically to indicate premises which are severally clear, distinct and certain; and to erect upon these premises a deductive system of thought. But the accurate expression of the final generalities is the goal of discussion and not its origin. Philosophy has been misled by the example of mathematics; and even in mathematics the statement of the ultimate logical principles is beset with difficulties, as yet insuperable. The verification of a rationalistic scheme is to be sought in its general success, and not in the peculiar certainty, or initial clarity, of its first principles.'

[1] See R. W. Clarke, op. cit., pp. 212–13.  [2] Ibid., p. 351.  [3] p. 10.

**E.** Just what the doctor ordered. It's a great pity Whitehead never read Hegel. Well, I hope we have now got fairly clear the difference between philosophic and scientific knowledge-and-ignorance.

**AE.** Yes, I think so. Your conception of knowledge and ignorance in philosophy made me think of Yeats's remark (I forget where): 'Man can embody truth, but he cannot know it.'

**E.** I would say man can know and embody truth in a degree, but for the same reason he can only know and embody it in a degree.

**AE.** Which makes him something of a paradox.

**E.** You wouldn't have me accept him as nothing but a spatio-temporal product of evolution, would you?

**AE.** No, and I'd like to go on discussing his oddness tomorrow.

# IV

## MAN

'I wish I loved the human race;
I wish I loved its silly face.'

'Man is Heaven's masterpiece.'

'Man is Nature's sole mistake.'

'Man is either a god or a beast.'

'Man is but a devil weakly fettered by some generous beliefs and impositions.'

'What a piece of work is man!'

'Man is a bundle of contradictions.'

Yes, and with yet more help from the *Oxford Dictionary of Quotations* we could considerably expand and further diversify this bundle of contradictory comments, all by highly intelligent writers. Most of them are clearly coloured by a passing mood and not considered verdicts; all the same, man, in commenting on himself, is under the difficulty which besets him *qua* a particle of the Absolute. Being only a particle, he is at once guaranteed against complete ignorance and precluded from complete knowledge.

As we agreed yesterday; but in this case?

By virtue of being a man he knows to a fair extent what men are like. He is self-conscious and capable of self-criticism, which means capable of criticizing humanity in himself and other men. He can draw on the social environment which largely determines him, and he may claim that nothing human is alien to him. Nevertheless he does not at all fully know himself, and he cannot objectify and comprehend mankind as a whole. And he doesn't get any better at it. I doubt whether any of us has as full a self-knowledge as Socrates had.

**AE.** Hard to verify.

 **E.** Yes, but I'm sure Montaigne and Shakespeare, four centuries ago, knew more about human nature than anybody today.

**AE.** Haven't the psychiatrists thrown any new light?

 **E.** They've produced some practical techniques which are sometimes effective, and of course the medical profession proper has long been accumulating knowledge of the human organism; a good doctor tends to know a lot about people. But these are practical men working among the sick. They are not concerned with the fulness of human nature. For that you must go to history, art, and literature, including of course the better philosophers, and to any spiritually important men and women whom you happen to know, or whom you may be able to observe.

**AE.** Because they are more real than their fellows?

 **E.** Precisely.

**AE.** What about the non-clinical psychologists?

 **E.** If you really want to know what the inside of a very distinguished man's mind is like you should read R. L. Stevenson's self-examinings in *An Inland Voyage*, and other intelligently introspective writings of the same kind. There is no true special science of the mind. The non-clinical psychologist is usually a behaviourist trying to explain it 'scientifically' as merely reaction to physical stimuli. Pavlov's salivating dog is the masterlight of all his seeing, and he gets passionately absorbed in rats running round mazes. It always astounds me that intelligent men can suppose the fascinating puzzle of mind and body soluble by cutting the knot and opting either for detachable immortal souls or for the crudest materialism. Nor does it help to fudge mind and matter together in neutral monism.

**AE.** All wrong ways to treat a good dilemma?

 **E.** Yes indeed. At the present time neither man nor the study of man seems to be making much progress. That might mend, but there is, as I said before we digressed, a fundamental difficulty. Man cannot objectify and comprehend mankind as a whole, not only because mankind is not a genuine whole and shows very little sign of becoming one, but also just because he is a man.

'What do they know of England who only England know?'

That's something like it.

Having no sufficiently effective contrast to himself to help him, man becomes too familiar with humanity in himself and his fellows. He has no adequate context in which to judge the human race.

That's it.

Would you say that, apart from his use or misuse of his senses, a man's possession of a body conditions both his knowledge and his ignorance of matter animate and inanimate?

I would, but not apart from the *use* of his senses. Without his body he couldn't have his knowledge-and-ignorance of dead and living matter, but a condition of his getting it is the presence in his body of dead matter and living sense organs.

So there is a sort of analogy here: to know spirit you must be spirit, and to be material is one condition of knowing matter. Yes I see. Could we now get away from the question whether the human race has been a triumph or a failure—we shall never know—and try to reflect philosophically on what an individual man is, admitting of course both that he is not fully real—that is why he must be in part material in order to know matter—and that we cannot hope to achieve more than quite inadequate knowledge shot through with ignorance?

So be it. I seize at once on the word 'individual', which should considerably develop its meaning as we proceed.

I have an inkling that the concrete universal is about to come into its own.

Maybe; albeit I want to start at the other end by suggesting that you touch very little of a man when you consider him as a singular individual.

That's pretty obvious. You mean, I suppose, a man as a statistical unit, a man not recognizably characterized but merely classified as a citizen of this or that state, as liable to military service, or entitled to a parliamentary vote or an old-age pension, or just as a numbered but anonymous prisoner in Siberia? In short the bureaucrat's view of humanity, not unakin to the sociologist's, and enshrined ridiculously in utilitarian ethics?

**E.** Oh yes; it ties up with every sort of empiricist attempt to aggregate a world out of singulars. Of course statistics have an indispensable practical use, but I fancy the habit of mind they engender fosters an unthinking egalitarianism, by which I mean the fallacy that just being a man entitles you to the same sized share of everything as every other man. It's symptomatic of this attitude that if you want somebody to have the courage of his opinions you don't, unless you are a militant revolutionary, tell him to get up and fight for them but 'to stand up and be counted'.

**AE.** Like a sheep or a trade-unionist.

**E.** Exactly. Now let's carry the search for man up the scale a bit.

**AE.** One question before you start. Are you going to say that men tend to lose their mere singularity as one gains more and more insight into their real natures? By 'singularity' I mean not idiosyncrasy but numerability. But surely even great men can be counted.

**E.** Yes, when somebody is selecting names for an encyclopedia. The point is that number means less and less as you go up from the world of Nature where things are less or more self-external.

**AE.** Self-external?

**E.** I borrow the term from Hegel. He does not usually contrast 'internal' and 'external' as meaning respectively inside and outside a spatial container. No doubt phrases in common parlance such as 'inmost thoughts' and 'inner feelings' recall a time when thoughts and feelings were supposed to be safely hidden in the head and the heart until you spoke or blushed. Hegel transforms the privacy of possession which this was supposed to confer to mean self-possessed and so concentrated individuality, contrasting it with loose dispersion, which *per contra* he called self-externality, *aussersichsein*. Thus I meant aggregates rather than wholes of mutually determining constituents.

. Rocks rather than radishes, in general plants rather than animals, at the bottom perhaps space and time as sheer dispersedness or self-externality. You take all that from Hegel?

. Yes I do. It explains, incidentally, why mathematics, as I said the other day, is poison if it creeps up into philosophy. Hegel's own illustration really does illuminate, whatever your theological views may be, when he says that the number three has a much more subordinate significance when we speak of God as a Trinity than it has when we consider the three dimensions of space or the three sides of a triangle.[1] One should bear that in mind when considering the triads of the dialectic. What tends to keep one thinking of men as singulars is the fact that each of them has a body.

. Would you say that the *an sich* of a live human body is not *für sich* but only *für uns*?

. That's rather a red herring, isn't it?

. You said at the beginning, before I came on, that we might on occasion meander; and I'm always intrigued by that Hegelian distinction.

. You are really asking, aren't you, whether a living human organism as such is a sufficiently genuine whole of mutually determining constituents (sufficiently 'individual' in the truer sense of the word) to be in some dim sort self-conscious?

. I suppose I am.

. Difficult, but perhaps not entirely irrelevant.

. Thank you.

. Let's try to think it out. A human body can be an object of all the five senses to its owner as well as to the rest of us. So you might think that in this respect it didn't differ from a corpse, and that its *an sich* was only *für uns*, 'for us', including among 'us' its owner. The behaviourists might agree with you, but you would be wrong. Being a sensible object even to its owner is not all that a living human body is. The sensating subject is the man himself, not just his body; but he sensates in, and I think we

---

[1] Cf. *Encyclopaedia*, §99, *Zusatz*, para 3.

may say as, his body. We agreed just now that being material is one condition of knowing matter. The sense organs are thus slightly more than the mere instruments which their name implies, and it might not be nonsense to say that there is a faint approximation to self-consciousness in a living human body as such.

**AE.** In other words all sense function is psychophysical, and body and mind (or soul or whatever you like to call spirit at this level) constitute a unity which somehow bestrides two distinguishable but inseparable levels of Being. You cannot split this unity into an immortal soul and a perishable body, nor into two parallel or interacting functions.

**E.** Nor, to complete the old traditional triad of hypotheses, is mind 'epiphenomenal'. Philosophy has got to accept this continuous lift from level to level throughout Nature and spirit. Natural science of necessity moves on the flat. Its observations and measurements cannot touch transcendence anywhere. That explains, too, why the modern empiricist philosopher, equally a worker on the flat, cannot as a rule, especially when confronted by art or conduct, produce anything but linguistical ingenuities.

**AE.** Then Hegel was right to try to build up the results of natural science into a philosophy of Nature?

**E.** Yes, and to carry it unbrokenly on into a philosophy of spirit.

**AE.** If mathematics and natural science provide material for philosophic speculation, their function cannot be, as Benedetto Croce held, solely utilitarian and in no degree contributory to theoretical truth.

**E.** No, it can't. I have a good deal of sympathy with Croce's view of the special sciences as purely 'economic' in purpose, largely because they are wholly unconcerned with intrinsic values; but on the whole I believe now that they do also reveal basic minimal characters of things which justify Hegel's dialectical theorizing of them. Without that I don't think I could make any sense of the roots of the human spirit in physical Nature. I should have to abandon the fascinating puzzle and opt either for materialism or for subjective idealism, and I find little attraction in either.

**℞.** You don't find Nature very real?

**℞.** I find it not unreal but not very real except aesthetically; though that is vastly important.

**℞.** Well let's get back to man. You are now going to show me how a man in his full nature, in such degree of reality, that is, as he is capable of attaining, is individual not *qua* singular, as his possession of a body or the entry of his name on a list might suggest, but as a whole of mutually determining elements; as a unity, in fact, not a unit? We might now call him a person?

**℞.** That's what I'll try to do, and we may certainly call him a person.

**℞.** I suspect you are going to say that the whole content of a person —spiritual, mental, psychical (I'm not trying to be terminologically exact), and physical so far as his body is a vehicle and so a constituent organ of spirit—is a concrete unity but not a unity rigidly bounded, so to say, within a ring fence. In fact I think you must say that if his individuality is to differ in kind from that of the atom in the aggregate or the monad.

**℞.** Yes; very far from rigidly bounded.

**℞.** Yet there are people who would individuate a man on the basis that not only does he own one body but his feelings are private and unshareable. They will perhaps even tell you that in all his experience a human being is basically alone.

**℞.** So blending subjectivism and pessimism. Doubtless feeling in its immediacy is unshareable, and I suppose coenaesthetic feeling pervades all or most human experience. But feeling mediated, the developed content of feeling, is eminently shareable.

**℞.** What exactly is the distinction?

**℞.** Well, take Aristotle's definition of an emotion as a case of form in matter: emotion, he says, is a logos, a judgement, embodied in *pathos*, feeling.[1]

**℞.** Analogous to Kant's conception of thought empty without sensuous intuition, and intuition blind without thought?

[1] *De Anima*, 403ᵃ 25, and cf. *Rhet.*, 1378a 31 ff.

**E.** More or less. The formal element, the logos, is universal and therefore shareable, however confusedly embodied in feeling it may be. I think you will agree that the emotion of a furiously indignant or wildly enthusiastic crowd is not simply an aggregation of its members' singular individual, private feelings. The emotion may be that of an intelligent audience rising to applaud the perfect singing of a Mozart aria, or it may be as abysmally crude as it was at a Nüremberg rally, but even in the latter case it must be informed by some sort of a logos. Feeling without any logos is, like Aristotle's primary matter, an ideal limit only approached closely in physical pain so intense that it can scarcely be located. That is why the emotivist doctrine of values is so utterly false. But now look above the feeling of a man tortured by intense pain, and above mere crowd emotion barely differntiated because the logos in it is so rudimentary. Look at the mutually constituent pairs we talked of yesterday: two lovers in the hottest flame of physical and imaginative, perhaps also intellectual, union; two dancers or two musical executants, joined not necessarily in any passion of love, but in sensitive comprehension of each other's sensitive movement, their interplay embraced within the music they interpret—would you deny that these share their feeling? Call it empathy if you like, but realize that its basis is a real identity. Would you deny that for the time being they find themselves in each other, and are thereby not diminished but transcended?

**AE.** No I wouldn't, but——

**E.** And why should we stop there? It may be that man's most intense felicities, if not his greatest achievements, are enjoyed in paired partnerships, but in all the human associations into which he enters, just by being born, or actively as he matures, there is a mutual determining. Where this is not recognized, ethical theory is bankrupt. A man gives himself and receives himself, and what cannot be determined is the extent to which his personality may extend in his lifetime or when he is dead. What limit is there to Homer or Dante? But of course——

**AE.** Stop! You get so carried away that I can't get an objection in edgeways, and, after all, that's partly what I'm here for. You are supposed to be building up the notion of an individual person as a concrete unity. I don't object to your swelling the content of him with all he draws from the contextual determining of his contemporaries, or from the dead who have taught him directly or indirectly most of what he knows. You may add what he gains from his imagination of men unborn whose hearts and minds he may hope to influence through the relics of him in one shape or another. But you are trying to include in the concrete unity of an individual person not only the good he does (to say nothing of the evil) which escapes interment with his bones, but the whole afterglow of his fame. You are indeed not confining him within a ring fence, but surely you disperse him so widely that he ceases to be an individual person at all.

Even if he flits live from lip to lip? Even if the whole earth is his tomb? Are there no 'heirs of all eternity'? Ennius spoke truth, and Pericles's funeral speech is not empty uplift. Go and read it again; then read again Diotima's speech in that unmatched masterpiece, Plato's *Symposium*. All recorded history refutes you. You are making as great a mistake as any empiricist. In fact you are making two mistakes. First, you will stick in the notion that individuality is a function of limitation, even if not of singularity. Of course expansion can dilute individuality, but not if it is genuine concretion of the individual; only if it comes in the form of not fully organic increment which destroys proportion, as obesity ruins the body's health and beauty, or as excessive versatility may make a man fritter his talent. Secondly, you are thinking of a man only as he is *für sich*. He is self-conscious and he may be self-critical, but the content of him in that aspect alone is only one element of him. Taken as the whole of him it is a mere caricature of his finitude. I should have thought that was common knowledge: 'O wad some Pow'r the giftie gie us', and so forth. A great man needs a biography as well as an autobiography. A man's opinion of himself, if it can be elicited, presents as a rule a highly corrigible picture.

And so may a woman's. I can't resist breaking in with a frivolous but apt illustration. I once switched on TV, and the picture came up before the sound. It was a close-up of the ugliest female face I ever saw. It was, I admit, one of those old horrendous BBC close-ups which used to reveal each pit and wrinkle, each spot and each superfluous hair, thereby turning the human cheek into a very fair semblance of the moon photographed from outer space; all the same she was a veritable gorgon. The face was working with strong emotion, and then rasping tones became audible. She was urging perfect promiscuity, sexual freedom unconfined, and she ended with a fierce tirade against male jealousy. The camera switched to a slightly shaken interviewer. 'But, Miss X', he said, 'did you ever meet a man you thought incapable of sexual jealousy?' Back went the camera. 'Oh yes!' replied Medusa with a deadly smirk, 'my husband. He's splendid. He's never jealous.' I achieved total laughter.

**E.** Marvellous! But of course there is a vast amount about himself or herself that no man or woman can possibly ever know. Humility as well as conceit can blind us to ourselves, and full self-knowledge in the ordinary acceptation of the term . . . well, Aristotle's great-souled man is under no delusions about himself, but he does somehow lack charm.

**AE.** Perhaps a little self-ignorance may, *pace* Socrates, be sometimes quite a good thing.

**E.** You're probably right. I've sometimes thought I would like to write my own obituary—'stock obit' they call it—for *The Times*, but I think perhaps I'd better not ask them if I may. But let me get on. The self, thus narrowly conceived, not only mistakes itself, but fluctuates in a tidal ebb and flow which becomes insanity in the manic depressive. This is easily perceptible in ordinary everyday life, if you attend to it. The clothes a woman wears when she wishes to please are a part of her, and at least in her own view she may very well dwindle when she takes them off. *Pars minima est ipsa puella sui*, as Ovid neatly put it. A bat may fuse psychically with the body of a cricketer hitting a six, and become a dead thing again when he's bowled and carries it back to the pavilion. A man may recover from sickness or despair and tell his friends, not purely metaphorically, that he is a new man or his old self again. But I labour the obvious. Philosophers have often argued about the basis of personal identity, looking at it from this narrow angle. One remembers Hume's thin and superficial discussion of it. Yet the view from this angle, though partial, is not irrelevant, especially in ethics.

I remember F. H. Bradley, when he was over seventy, telling me that if he were persuaded by evidence that as a young man he had done something wicked which he had quite forgotten, he would not now accept moral responsibility for it, because he no longer had any feeling of identity with himself as an undergraduate. But mark you this. It was Bradley who said in *What is the real Julius Caesar?*, 'We must treat the individual as real so far as anywhere for any purpose his being is appreciable.'

I see the difference. You'll somehow have to synthesize the two points of view, but before you try to do that I want to raise a question. Your tale of Bradley and his conscience makes me wonder whether a man *qua* moral agent is not more individual by limitation than he is *qua* poet or philosopher. In his acceptance of responsibility, in his loyalty to his own conscience, the morally good man, I suggest, is nearer to being a singular individual than he is as a thinker or an artist. Is he not praised or blamed for particular actions much more minutely than they are for their particular productions?

In the nursery or the school reward and punishment must follow particular actions more or less closely. In a criminal court the verdict can only label the accused guilty or not guilty of a particular act or acts. This insistence on particular acts is obviously indispensable for the maintenance of law and order, but although a judge is sometimes heard to remind a jury that the court over which he presides is not a court of morals, the legal attitude has been apt to spread beyond the law. It has found its way into such ethical theories, ancient or modern, as would rest moral worth on rules mainly negative. Thinkers thus persuaded, whether puritanically or casuistically inclined, tend to concentrate their arguments on the singular act rather than on a man's whole moral policy, so to say, his whole way of life. It's excusable if you are trying to teach men how to behave, as was Aristotle in his *Ethics*, but it is hopelessly cramping in philosophical theory, and it doesn't make for charity in everyday life.

We should, you mean, as philosophers and even as good neighbours allow a man some measure of concrete universality. Of course the wider view implies that morality is not absolute, as the puritan would like to think it, and that our moral criterion, like all other human criteria, must remain imprecise. If we hold that a man gains content from, but is also determined by, a variety of context, hereditary and environmental, and is not, so far as we can judge, free of contingency, then we can only decide roughly the degree of his responsibility. Hence, I suppose, myths of Rhadamanthus or any other final judge who might possibly give us a second chance. Hence also, in our sceptical age, the squeamishness rather than compassion which made us abolish capital punishment. Moreover, when I say, 'not free of contingency so far as we can judge', I don't mean to impute the element of contingency merely to ignorance. I mean that morality cannot in essence be more than a constituent approximation to absolute spirit.

**E.** That was to be expected. Meanwhile we must return from this meander in morality to the business of putting together what we see of ourselves with what others see of us. Tomorrow I will try to be more philosophically serious, but I'd like to finish today's talk by remarking on one field where they very vividly supplement one another. I mean drama, and in particular the plays of Shakespeare.

**AE.** Splendid. I thought perhaps you were going to try to put together the Winston Churchill of his autobiographical works with the comments of his friends and enemies which Martin Gilbert is recording as he produces the biography. The synthesis is already fascinating, but I would sooner meander with you in Shakespeare. It is a world which I am always loth to leave.

**E.** Good. I start here from Hamlet's (and clearly Shakespeare's) very decisively announced view that the purpose of drama is not parody or escapism but the expansion and deepening of man's self-consciousness. The quotation is hackneyed but ever memorable: 'Playing, whose end, both at the first and now, was, and is, to hold as t'were the mirror up to Nature; to show virtue her own feature, scorn her own image, and the very age and body of the time, his form and pressure.' And now the technique for doing it. You'll agree that any leading character in a play is expressed not only by what he does and says to the others, but also by what is said about him and said and done to him. The dramatist has to synthesize the two aspects.

Three really, if you're talking about Shakespeare. You must add the soliloquies, at any rate those which Nevill Coghill classifies under 'Personal epiphany' in his admirable chapter on the subject in *Shakespeare's Professional Skills*.

Direct self-portraiture is a vital and skilfully used instrument in Shakespeare's presentation of character, but I was thinking of his more indirect and subtle method, which he reveals quite incidentally when he makes Ulysses in *Troilus and Cressida* try to stir the sulking Achilles to action:

> That man, however dearly parted,
> How much in having, or without or in,
> Cannot make boast to have that which he hath,
> Nor feels not what he owes but by reflection;
> As when his virtues shining upon others
> Heat them, and they retort that heat again
> To the first giver.

He uses this technique especially in presenting his women, possibly to help his boy actors. Cleopatra, as her fortunes sink, rises to a height of royal splendour in poetry which is in effect beyond the powers of any actress—was it really tolerable to listen to an adolescent 'boying her greatness' at the Globe?— yet much glory reflects on her also from the few marvellous lines given to Iras and Charmian.

And how the cynical Enobarbus builds her up earlier in the play! He knows perfectly well what an actress she is: 'Cleopatra, catching but the least noise of this, dies instantly; I have seen her die twenty times upon far poorer moment.'

Even Antony, wondering how on earth he is going to get away to Rome, then admits, 'She's cunning past man's thought.'

But Enobarbus was not too cynical to be dazzled by the barge on the Cydnus, the most lingering picture Shakespeare ever painted; and it is he who pays the famous tribute, 'Age cannot wither her' and so forth.

But he cannot resist ending it with a touch of satire:

> Vilest things
> Become themselves in her, that the holy priests
> Bless her when she is riggish.

That is not, I think, in Plutarch.

**AE.** Enobarbus perfectly mirrors the whole tragedy with his ironic comment and his final suicide. But I wonder whether Imogen in *Cymbeline* isn't a yet better example than Cleopatra of Shakespeare's cross-lighting. She has plenty to say for herself, especially in her superb scene with Pisanio when she learns that her husband has ordered him to kill her.

**E.** I've always regarded Posthumus in *Cymbeline* and Claudio in *Much Ado* as insufferable cads as well as perfect fools.

**AE.** Hear, hear. Shakespeare did now and again concede too much to the plots he took over. Posthumus is damned *a priori* by the plot, and Shakespeare, to my mind, fails dismally to blow him up into a magnificent chap by means of extravagant praise in the mouths of other characters. Shakespeare, however, was a busy man. But don't interrupt. I was going to say that you get a quite magical light thrown on the infinitely charming Imogen when Belarius's two boys fall in love with Fidele at first sight. Iachimo, stealing out of the trunk, has shown us her physical beauty, and the whole cave-dwelling episode, with its strange out-of-the-world atmosphere, is an exaltation of her irresistibly sweet nature. In the funeral rites her unknown brothers' tender feeling for her culminates with marvellous poignancy, although we know she isn't dead.

**E.** Those boys, growing up to virtue in isolation and innocence, rather like Miranda—one feels at first that their affection for Fidele is going to be a shade mawkish.

**AE.** But lest you should have supposed anything of the sort: 'Re-enter Guiderius with Cloten's head.'

**E.** Quite. I'd like to finish with what might be the best example of the lot, the showing forth of Perdita in *Winter's Tale*. She is my favourite among Shakespeare's virgins, and I rather fancy, *pace* a few dessicated eighteenth-century minds like Pope and Johnson, that it is the greatest of Shakespeare's comedies. Certainly it is the most passionate, and it is immensely effective on the stage.

Hazlitt admired it.

Oh of course he did. When Hazlitt wrote, poetry had become poetry again. He is the best critic of Shakespeare, indeed of all the English poets he knew, and he had a healthy contempt for Johnson in that capacity. I have a feeling that his own lively and imaginative style was a good deal moulded by reading Shakespeare. Coleridge may have helped, but he is vastly more lucid than S.T.C. in prose.

Agreed. Shakespeare was certainly a constituent of Hazlitt. But we mustn't wander too far. What exactly do you mean by the 'showing forth' of Perdita?

I mean in effect Act iv scene iii, which begins with her first appearance since she was a newborn babe in Act ii. She sits 'most goddess-like pranked up' in her fancy dress as mistress of the feast, drinking in the compliments of the totally enamoured and adoring Florizel, but a little embarrassed by her contrast with her badly dressed lover, which seems to reverse their relative social positions. Despite the staunchness of Florizel, she has fears, too, like Juliet, for the future of their loves. She is slightly dazed when her foster-father bustles her into welcoming the unknown friends. But she is a princess, and she pulls herself together. By a lucky chance Dorcas is passing with a basket of flowers. She stops her and takes handfuls. They inspire her to a floral eloquence not surpassed for beauty elsewhere in Shakespeare. They lift her at last into an almost ecstatic declaration of her love:

> Per.                    O these I lack
> To make you garlands of; and my sweet friend,
> To strew him o'er and o'er.
> Flo.                    What? Like a corse?
> Per. No, like a bank for love to lie and play on;
> Not like a corse: or if,—not to be buried,
> But quick, and in mine arms.

For a moment the spell breaks:

> Methinks I play as I have seen them do
> In whitsun pastorals: sure, this robe of mine
> Does change my disposition.

By this time Polixenes and Camillo are amazed and enchanted.

Then she shines in Florizel's rapturous praise: 'What you do/ Still betters what is done', etc. They all do homage. Even Polixenes, in his rage when he discovers that they really mean to marry without consulting him, addresses Perdita as 'enchantment'. She is thereafter much enhanced by Florizel's immovable constancy, because she so clearly merits it.

**AE.** When they reach Sicilia she glows again in the instant flame of admiration and love which she kindles in everyone she meets. The only exception is the valiant lioness Paulina, ever jealously defending the perfections of Hermione. The wildly enthusiastic poetical Gentleman who announces Perdita's arrival is sharply snubbed for disloyalty to his former queen:

> She had not been,
> Nor was not to be equalled; thus your verse
> Flowed with her beauty once: 'tis shrewdly ebbed,
> To say you have seen a better.

Even when she has herself seen Perdita she remains unimpressed and rebukes the already enchanted Leontes:

> Sir, my liege,
> Your eye hath too much youth in't,

and the poor man has to say he was thinking of Hermione all the time, which of course he wasn't. But when Paulina realized that Perdita was Hermione's daughter, then, by the report of perhaps the same Gentleman, 'She lifted the princess from the earth; and so locked her in embracing, as if she would pin her to her heart, that she might be no more in danger of losing.'

**E.** That was subtle psychology.

**AE.** No it wasn't. It was all just what Paulina's generous and fiercely energetic nature dictated. She was *bound* to lift Perdita off her feet and hug her. 'Subtle' suggests deliberate manipulation, which was seldom Shakespeare's way. Unless the exigencies of a borrowed plot constrain him, he doesn't manipulate, he creates. Not for nothing did Balzac, greatest of novelists, call Shakespeare the greatest of creators after God. His characters are not his puppets; he engenders in them a power or a weakness, a virtue or a vice, from which their words and deeds flow freely self-determining. That is why every line of his best poetry, a pretty high proportion, brings a shock of surprise which turns instantly to the recognition of an inevitability as natural as a sunrise.

**E.** Paulina-like you rebuke me, and justly. What you say is true of all great art. The flash of creation shocks one's dull mind of the moment into delighted acceptance. It changes one's world. But we have meandered enough. I think we have shewn how Shakespeare could blend inner consciousness and outer aspect to create a human being, but tomorrow we must try to be more explicitly philosophical.

**E.** But I *did* enjoy the meander, and before we part a point occurs to me about Shakespeare's method of displaying character, an exception which really does go to prove our rule. Hamlet is so dominated by his introvert's habit of agonizing self-analysis that we need no further illuminant. Apart from a few lines from Ophelia and a line from Fortinbras, no other character throws any light on Hamlet the man. His true nature is veiled from all but the discreetly reticent Horatio.

# V

## MAN AS UNIVERSAL

**E.** Today I would like to talk about the universality of a man. But I warn you that, despite what I thought was a fruitful talk about the concrete universal three days ago, I am still not at my ease when I discuss the universal. I become very conscious of my ignorance overlapping my knowledge. I long then for a ποῦ στῶ, a solid platform to think from, though I know it is a quite unphilosophical hankering.

**AE.** You sometimes wish you could be watching the game from the side-lines with Wittgenstein, or that you were safely chained among Plato's cave-dwellers and could observe the shadows shifting on the wall without any fear that there was something wrong with the 'cognitive situation'?

**E.** Precisely.

**AE.** You would have plenty of fellow troglodytes; yesterday's bureaucrats, for example, viewing men as singular individuals. You might also find——

**E.** Hush. We shall never get on if we start incarcerating our colleagues in the Cave as Dante dumped his enemies in Hell.

**AE.** All right, but we might begin there and work our way up.

**E.** What notion of the universal would you say the cave-dwellers have?

**AE.** Not much, but Plato does suggest that they might hold competitions, and give prizes to those who were most successful in remembering what things usually came first and what second, and so were good at guessing the future. That implies apprehension of the universal as a common character definite enough to be recognizably repetitive. It is significant that the 'firsts' and the 'seconds' are not linked causally. All the prisoners can do in the way of thinking is to classify singulars which they recognize as turning up in an ordered succession.

**E.** Very Russellian. His ghost I do see sitting there, shivering the shadows into multiplicities of sense-data. I'm afraid that you and I cannot consent to be comfortably chained. We have declared that a man is a great deal more than an aggregate of classifiable singulars. We cannot join the empiricists in endeavouring so completely to absorb and exhaust the universal in its instances that only singular individuals emerge as real. Our universal takes its nature from the universe. The empiricists are perfectly right in trying to absorb the universal in the individual, but they fail to see that the individual in which the universal is consummated is not singular.

**E.** And so back to the concrete universal. But here I have one or two comments to make. In the first place the universal which is concreted or consummated in the individual cannot be a sheerly simple quality, any more than the individual in which it is concreted can be a sheer singular. Otherwise we should be left with nothing but a second multiplicity of logically indiscriminable units.

**E.** I entirely agree. It is no use multiplying simple qualities and saying that several universals together consummate themselves in this or that individual. The universal must differentiate itself specifically as it moves from general to individual. In fact it is as wrong to pluralize the universal as it is to singularize the individual.

**E.** True enough if we were talking directly of the concrete universal as a self-definition of absolute spirit, but actually we are talking of its finite constituents, and we had to admit some time ago that they have only a degree of truth and reality. Surely the objects of pictorial thinking are inevitably judged as instantiating a severality of quite loosely linked universal qualities which constitute not a genuinely concrete individual but something much more like a singular individual. At that level generality and singularity must live in an uneasy but indissoluble partnership. Need I remind you of that pungent, white, cubic lump of salt with which Hegel illustrates the category of Thinghood? Indeed, if in Hegel's *Logic* one descends from Absolute Idea to

Pure Being, or in the *Philosophy of Spirit* from Philosophy to Natural Soul, or in Nature from Animal Organism to Time and the *partes extra partes* of Space, each step is a decline in concrete universality, a steady lapse of the truly individual towards the self-external.

**E.** Oh yes, I would have said all that given time. Since we are on the subject, I will add that on the strength of this lapse into self-externality, this sprawling self-dispersedness which characterizes the ideality of the finite at these low levels, Hegel charges Nature with impotence; and he admits a streak of contingency not only in Nature but also in human affairs. Contingency (*Zufälligkeit*) is what might be otherwise than as it is, and the contingent differs from the possible only because it happens to *be*. In human conduct it is caprice (*Willkür*).

**AE.** I suppose that answers my question of the other day as to how we are able to think impossibles hypothetically.[1] Incidentally, this sending of time and space to the bottom of the queue, so to speak, on the ground of their hopeless lack of individuality suggests that they have a literally minimal significance in determining the nature of anything which really matters.

**E.** Yes; they are indefinitely regressive, the very nadir of self-externality in the finite. They have for Hegel only enough individuality to synthesize in Matter-and-motion. On the other hand, they are forms of sensuous inuition and they persist as media in any experience in which sense is not wholly transcended. What you will not discover from Hegel or anyone else is why they should be what they are.

**AE.** That is the point for which we gave Spinoza credit three days ago,[2] but it is part of a much wider, unanswerable question. Let's return now to our muttons, suitably humbled by trying to look our faceless ignorance in the face. I take it that degrees of truth and reality, degress of *Wahrheit*, now appear as degrees of concrete universality, or true individuality? In proportion to the failure of true individuality, the universal appears to us as more merely general, more abstract, and the individual as more nearly a bare singular, more significantly countable?

---

[1] See p. 16, above.  [2] See pp. 26–7, above.

You say 'appears to us', but remember that we are not sitting in Plato's cave perceiving what we take to be independent things. We have eschewed both realism and phenomenalism. We affirm ourselves to be a semi-real constituent among other semi-real constituents of absolute spirit. Our knowledge shot with ignorance comes from this participation; it is not the fruit of observation from a solid platform, even if we wish it were. Our 'cognitive situation' is always ambivalent. I was saying just now that Hegel admits an element of contingency in Nature and human affairs, and the problem of contingency is a good example of this ambivalence. When we say that there is an element of contingency in Nature and human affairs, do we mean that there is some really random behaviour in things and men? Or do we believe that when we appeal to contingency, chance, random behaviour and so forth we are snatching a cloak to cover our ignorance?

I would have thought that, philosophically, an objective idealist must take contingency and ignorance as distincts never wholly separable which together constitute a low degree of *Wahrheit*. But to deny that they ever fall apart at all would leave no room for error, and we do sometimes decide that what at first seemed fortuitous had a necessitating cause. I don't feel very clear about it, but surely the dilemma should mainly worry the special scientist, who has commonly assumed in the past that he observes from a solid platform. He used to plump for ubiquitous *a tergo* necessitation, and the patches of random behaviour which the modern physicist inclines to admit look a bit odd juxtaposed to the necessitated within one system. Still, the unpredictable may somehow help him to predict, which is his main business, as it was the main business of the cave-dwellers. For all you and I know, it may herald an over-all change in physical theory. Could it be that physics has reached down to a new type of behaviour in the subatomic, a yet greater degree of self-externality which would relate analogously to mechanism as mechanism relates to organism?

If the physicists do decide that this is the answer, some philosophizing physicist is sure to tell us that this is the level where truth is to be found, the new bottom of the well.

**AE.** But for Hegel Nature and man are not independent objects laid out on a plate for observation, as they are for the special scientist, but phases of varying reality in the return upon itself of absolute spirit. I suppose really that if one accepts this notion of degrees of *Wahrheit*, of reality and truth (remembering that a degree of truth is as much a degree of ignorance as a degree of heat is a degree of cold) then Hegel's doctrine of contingency becomes pretty plausible: contingency and rigid *a tergo* necessitation are contradictories which are bound to puzzle the scientist, but synthesize in free necessity, rational self-determination, at a higher level.

**E.** Yes, I think Hegel answers the question as well as it can be answered. If one means to philosophize one must neither continue to hanker after a fixed observation post, nor cling to the faith that one has a right little tight little core of singular self-identity which will stay fixed through all we think and do and suffer. These are twin beliefs, useful maybe to practice but in philosophy delusive. Let's now get back to man.

**AE.** Let me try to summarize our position so far. The true individual is not the singular. If it were, an individual man would shrink absurdly into an arithmetical unit. The true individual is not the windowless Leibnizian monad, which contains internal diversity, as a true individual must, and is also individual by exclusion as any finite individual is bound contradictorily to be. But the two moments of individuality remain severed. The monad owes its content of internal diversity to a quite external and arbitary act of creation and pre-establishment by God, and monads accordingly can only be aggregated; they cannot of their own nature enter into a concrete unity. The whole which contains them can only be their sum.

**E.** The Leibnizian monadology, like the solipsistic position, is a very instructive impossibility.

**AE.** True individuality, we think, depends on the amplitude of the universal moment concreted in the individual, but there is a half-truth in the monad. Only the Absolute, *qua* wholly self-othering, can be conceived as fully individual. A man cannot be absolutely individual, and to the extent to which he fails he is individual by exclusion. This makes him a contradiction. As he fails fully to contain his other, so proportionately the universal in him fails of concreteness and remains relatively general. He then shares qualities with other men, and if that were not so he and they would simply and absurdly not exist. He *is* a contradiction.

True enough, but so is everything finite. A man is nevertheless much more importantly individual by virtue of what he includes. That is one reason I don't favour doctrines of the singular immortal soul. Of course a man has a context of other men, and you may say that he excludes them; but he draws something of his own nature from all the various communities of which he is at all an organic member, and he contributes something to them. What is in a sense exclusion is a reciprocal relation—of course in varying degree. And is it fanciful to think, as I suggested the day before yesterday, that there is still a reciprocal determining when a great man of the past has affected the course of history, and the historian labours to re-think his thoughts and understand his actions, and so to present him truly as he was and is?

You said before that even if and when the human race perishes, man's persisting reality has in it a dimension of eternity, though you have made it very clear that you do not believe in detachable immortal souls.

I'm sure it has. If creation *ex nihilo* is impossible, as it obviously is, then so is total dissolution *in nihilum*. If time in no way at all implies eternity, life becomes a far too idiotic and insignificant tale to make it worthwhile to try to philosophize about it. But I'd rather talk of that later.

May we, then, dwell a little on a man's survival—or perhaps I should say growth or diminution—in the minds of the generations which succeed him? When the historians decide to re-write history and proceed to whitewash Richard III or Philippe le Bel, or to blacken the memory of Louis XIV or Elizabeth I, or when the critics attempt to revalue the poetry of Chaucer or John Donne, what bearing has that on the *Being* of those worthy or unworthy persons?

Common sense would say, I suppose, none at all. Let's see how the common-sense view works out. The man dies and ceases to

be. Memories of him, surviving effects which he caused such as
the son he begot and the fortune he left him, the cathedral he
built, his philosophy and his poetry, and the political revolution
he inspired—all these without difference of degree are severed
from him, and if they now exist they exist on their own. They
cannot enter into his present being because he has no present
being. Some elements of some of them belonged to his past
being, but even if it be admitted that the past has some sort of
existence now, this is quite unalterable: death finally sums a
man's being. Perhaps one has to admit that the past has some
sort of being now, because memory must have an object, but
this present-past cannot now itself change, and the revised views
of historians and critics are at best only subjective correction of
our records.

**AE.** The death-bed spectacle has a terrifying finality. The attitude
you describe stems, maybe, from the agonizing sense of utter
loss which comes when death cuts a strong bond of love. Then
men try to calm the pain of it and mitigate their own shrinking
from extinction with this or that myth of an after-life.

**E.** Much poetry has sprung from the grief of bereavement and the
passionate refusal to accept death as sheer annihilation. How
varied the poets' response to death has been. Lucretius, armour-
plated in scientific atomism, scorns superstition and lament
for death: *Quid mortem congemis ac fles?*

**AE.** Cornelia in that so touching poem of Propertius breathes
resignation:

> *Desine, Paulle, meum lacrimis urgere sepulcrum;*
> *Panditur ad nullas janua nigra preces.*

**E.** Milton augurs for Lycidas the normal destiny of a good
Christian. Through the tepid stanzas of *In Memoriam* Tennyson
remains in honest doubt. But the death of Keats drew from
Shelley no dull outpouring on an abstract theme but his
noblest and most passionate verse; and in Shelley's pantheism
there at least are better grounds for a great poet's immortality
than in the attribution of a singular detachable soul:

> He is made one with Nature: there is heard
> His voice in all her music, from the moan
> Of thunder, to the song of night's sweet bird.

**:.** Last Post and Reveille do indeed mean different things to different men. To return to your common-sense attitude; I would say it is vulnerable without recourse to criticizing singular souls. As you describe it, the dead man's being is seen as (*a*) a self-subsistent present existence in the shape of what he has effected, which is quite cut off from his deceased person, and (*b*) an immutably embalmed past of him somehow existing now in order to provide memory with an object. Time confuses us all when we try to think about it, because space and time, though they are our constant companions, are the most primitive elements in our experience and the most distant from thought. Nevertheless this impossibly crude common-sense attempt to relate past and present confounds confusion worse. As soon as you insist on a sharp division between past and present you reduce the absolutely present to an abstract instant without duration. You are then forced to accept your experience as a specious present in which presentness lapses gradually into pastness. Present and past are seen as analogous to heat and cold: a degree of one is an inverse degree of the other.

**:.** At least that keeps the temporal show continuous in development or decay. You seem to be borrowing from William James and moving towards Croce's view of all history as contemporary history. What about the future?

**:.** Time present and past we apprehend as immanent in the change-and-rest which we use it to measure. To that extent it may be said to have a content as *durée*. But one can scarcely say that the future has a content. It has being, or rather not-being, as the object not of thought but of hope and fear. One can't, on the other hand, image, think of—what am I to say?—the past and present without the future.

**:.** You wouldn't allow the specious present a Jamesian 'forward fringe' and the future a content of contingent, merely possible, Being? That seems to be implied in Aristotle's not very firm view that today a particular future event must either be or not be about to occur tomorrow, yet neither must be nor must not be about to occur tomorrow; but when it has occurred or not occurred, hindsight can in principle trace a chain of necessary causation to its presence or absence.[1] There are the elements of contingency and necessitation which Hegel tried to synthesize.[2]

**AE.** The three dimensions of time, in which we commonly feel ourselves so inextricably bound up, present us with a no more than minimally intelligible object. Possibly we *can* only grasp time, or rather what occurs in time, as moving to a future whose contingency is perpetually cancelled in causation. But I am not sure that one can talk about time at all without begging the question. One is always finding oneself qualifying the past and the future as if they were present.

**E.** Don't despair. The best people have confessed themselves defeated by the problem of time. I expect no better success, but that doesn't excuse one from trying. Where shall we begin?

**AE.** With the Greeks. Plato in the *Timaeus* called time the moving image of eternity.

**E.** Aristotle said it was the number, the countable factor, by which change is measured. I am sure Plato was right both to contrast and to connect time with eternity, yet I fancy Aristotle was nearer the mark. If time *measures* change-and-rest, as it obviously does, it cannot itself move.

**AE.** And therefore cannot vary in pace, cannot gallop or amble, as Rosalind suggested to Orlando.

**E.** No, it has no speed. She confuses it as most of us do, when we aren't thinking with the change it measures. Aristotle puts it well. Time, he says, is not change, but it can't exist without change. It is a property of change. They define each other, and we use each to measure the other. Time is unending in either direction, past or future; it never came to be nor can it ever perish.

**AE.** Can you produce references for all that?

**E.** I could, but you'll find it all clearly set out in Bonitz's incomparable Index to Aristotle.

**AE.** What about eternity?

---

[1] Cf. *De Interpretatione*, Ch. 9.  [2] See p. 74, above.

E. Aristotle says that the things which always are, τὰ ἀεὶ ὄντα are not in time. Despite the *prima facie* meaning of the Greek words, he is clearly distinguishing the eternal not only from the transient in time but also from the everlasting.

E. I see. Aristotle separates eternal things from the spatio-temporal world of change which strives to assimilate itself to their independent eternity, by imitating it in degrees of cyclical movement; the relation is not reciprocal. But for Hegel, and presumably for you, the eternal as a moment of absolute spirit must be immanent in the world of rest-and-change which time measures. Time and the eternal must be somehow related as mutually self-constituent. I find that puzzling. Can you help me?

E. I'll try. To begin with, don't overemphasize Aristotle's separation of the timeless and the temporal. He regards all change teleologically. It is, he thinks, a development towards, or a decline from, a climactic end ordained by Nature. Having not fully severed special science from philosophy, he takes a teleological view of every process in the world of space and time from human affairs down to the fall of a stone, which is simply a case of earth unconsciously seeking its natural place as the lowest of the elements. But the degree to which the end is immanent varies in the various types of change. If the end aimed at were fully immanent at any and every instant of the process, change would have been superseded by timeless activity, and Aristotle does suppose man capable, or almost capable, of such activity.

E. I remember that at the end of our talk on monism you used Aristotle's notion of activity to illustrate the timeless movement of Absolute Idea.[1] Could you exemplify this doctrine, which seems pretty important?

E. The obvious example in the human sphere is Aristotle's distinction between (*a*) technical making, where the end is not immanent but a product which falls outside the process. Shoemaking, for instance, has no intrinsic value, and the shoemaker is judged good or bad solely according to the goodness or badness of his shoes; (*b*) moral conduct, which has an end beyond its process, but does to some extent qualify the agent as morally

---

[1] Cf. p. 34, above.

good or bad apart from his actual achievement; (*c*) the supreme happiness of the theoretic life, the value of which is purely intrinsic. How far the activity of (*c*) may transcend time rather depends on the status of Aristotle's νοῦς, a problem beyond us here.

**AE.** This variation in the immanence of the end seems to match the scale of degree and kind in Hegel between the self-external and, the concrete individual.

**E.** Yes, Hegel's Scale might be called the dynamic aspect of Aristotle's. In Aristotle, too, the immanence of the end in the process diminishes as we descend through Nature.

**AE.** I can understand types of change rising to activity on a scale of gradual immanence, but I still don't quite see how time is contained within Hegel's absolute spirit.

**E.** Hegel tries to display his hierarchical universe in all its aspects, and to relate the aspects in a dialectical hierarchy. I think we must here appeal to the Logic. Surely the relation of time to eternity is that of the spurious to the true infinite. These appear together quite early in Hegel's Logic among the categories of Quality. We may have to talk about them again later, but they are so important that repetition will do no harm. 'Quality' in Hegel is the thought, the definition, of Being as still so indeterminate, still so little developed beyond Pure Being, that it has as yet no quantitative character. You can only think it as a 'Somewhat'; even to give it the indefinite article is to speak proleptically. But with Somewhat begins finitude and its ideality. Somewhat, like every other positive category, begets its own negation, develops an other self. You are forced to think of Somewhat as *a* Somewhat with and against another Somewhat. But the second Somewhat is equally self-othering, and so is the third and so forth. Somewhat thus begets an unending series, prefiguring the ideality of finite things, and Hegel calls it the spurious infinite. But this unending series is after all at each step the re-instatement of the initial Somewhat, which thus returns upon itself and in this return becomes the True Infinite. Thus the true infinite contains the spurious infinite as a moment of itself, an approximative element *within it*. Hegel more than once points out (and it is most vital to his whole philosophy) that if you postulate a finite *outside* the true infinite, the latter at once becomes finite.

**E.** The containing of the finite in the infinite really epitomizes Hegel's system. Yet I'm still not happy about time, if you'll forgive the *naïveté* of the remark.

**E.** Space and time are, according to Hegel, the first and barest conceptual determinations (*Begriffsbestimmungen*) of Nature. There surely is the spurious infinite in which the logical category of spurious infinitude is concreted, obtains external Being.

**E.** But in the Logic, as you've just pointed out, the True Infinite emerges as *at once* sublating the spurious. Is there any analogue of that in Nature? Space and time synthesize in matter-and-motion which doesn't seem to me to concrete True Infinity in any way.

**E.** If, as seemed likely in our first talk, we apprehend space and time as wholes or quasi-wholes which we limit in grasping this or that particular extent or duration,[1] may not that wholeness or quasi-wholeness be the first concretion of the logical True Infinite, which appears as so early and primitive a category in the Logic? At every stage of Hegel's whole system what reveals itself is a system, a world or the adumbration of a world. Even the phases, the *Begriffsbestimmungen*, of Nature are phases of the concrete universal, not just generalizations without a unity.

**E.** You could be right.

**E.** Anyhow that's as far as I can get in trying to think about time.

**E.** There is one point which seems to emerge from this discussion, though it only confirms what we agreed before. If in experiencing temporal process we hold past and present events together in a coherent unity, it means that our consciousness of that unity cannot itself be no more than an event in time. It must in some sense belong to the things which always are.

**E.** As T. H. Green very soundly argued. But we do live in time as well as transcend it, and just how time subserves eternity we shall never know. Meanwhile we have wandered from the direct

---

[1] See p. 12. above.

question of a man's real persistence in time. I hope you will now admit that *sunt aliquid manes*, not as mere Propertian dream-visions but as a real development of at least some human beings beyond the grave.

**AE.** On the whole you persuade me, but I think we should here supplement our expansion of a man's individuality by recalling a central aspect of it, which we have rather neglected. I mean the fact that his main activities, his aesthetic, intellectual, economic, and moral activities, or however you like to distinguish them, are interpenetrant and overlapping; so that he enters whole into every jot and tittle of at any rate his fully conscious experience. He is *responsible*, morally, intellectually, and aesthetically.

**E.** That destroys the old myth of separate faculties, and it doesn't make it easy to maintain boundaries between different philosophical fields, but it is certainly true. If a man is a genuine individual, a concretely universal human being, he is a whole, and he is universal not merely as a purely general subject, i.e. not as merely a man who can say 'I' as can every other man by virtue of an abstract Kantian unity of apperception, but as a concrete person, a committed accomplice, self-differentiated in all the detail of his self-conscious living.

**AE.** One most easily perceives his individuality in the work of a philosopher or an artist. You get sharp transient impressions of a practical man, but his achievement is far harder to grasp as a coherent whole. It is less continuously under his control, and it is apt to sprawl and ramify elusively. The work of a scientist, and even more that of a mathematician, seems quite impersonal, devoid of style save in terms of clarity and distinctness. It is not easy to see how he goes whole into it, but somehow I suppose he does. On the other hand, the work of a great painter, poet, or composer vibrates throughout with its author's personality.

**E.** And each genuine work of art has its own individuality within the creating mind of its maker.

**AE.** Within it's maker's mind, yes. Benedetto Croce, regarding a work of art as an active intuition-expression, would so totally subject to the intuitive form any conceptual universal elements which it contains, that its unique individuality seems to make it a monad severed even from its creator and his other works. In the first chapter of the *Estetica* he aks, 'Who ever looked at a landscape painting and thought of space' (which Croce calls a category), 'unless reflection broke in on his contemplation?' Perhaps nobody, but I am quite sure that when I look at a Turner landscape or a Monet I am conscious within my contemplation that this is a Turner or a Monet. When I listen to a Mozart piano concerto I don't need an irruption of reflection to sense Mozart. To me it is the man in his works and his works in the man which count, and that has nothing at all to do with his private life. Of all the facts lost to history the ones I least regret are those of the life of Homer and what we don't know about the life of Shakespeare. The poet or the artist is to me a world within which I enjoy the particular work. And if I'm dwelling too much on appreciation rather than creation, I believe, let me say, that the artist's intuition-expression comes to be out of an operative context of which he is in some degree conscious, however sudden a birth it may seem. Nor am I at all sure—artists don't tell me so—that he always achieves concrete unity in a flash before he gets to work with the material tools of his trade. And when Croce degrades the physical work of art to a mere economic means of communication I feel it is like saying that minds have no bodies.

B. You may well be right. I suppose Croce would have replied that the Monet or Mozart quality was a conceptual element transformed to content in your intuition. One has to remember that Croce will admit in philosophy no tinge of the empirical and no transcendence. For us only the Absolute is fully concrete universal, and if Croce wants absolute individuality he must find his own place for it. Again, I feel a doubt about that pure isolation indicated in the denial that anybody looking at a landscape painting thinks about space unless reflection breaks in. I am inclined to believe that when I look at sculpture or painting or read a poem, I am feeling a tension, though perhaps faintly, between the imagined but more real world of the work of art and the 'real' world of everyday experience, a world which is neither copied nor distorted nor feigned in art, but transcended. If it is a landscape, say a Constable, I don't stop and think about space, but I do believe that within my aesthetic experience of the moment I am feeling, here is common East Anglian space glorified. And think of the great portraitist, who only succeeds because he has the power to include 'what isn't there'. I would say that, alike as creator and appreciator, a man enters the world of art, not with the suddenness of change in a dream, but with the consciousness of transcendence.

**AE.** You remind me of some remarks which Keats makes in a letter to his brother: 'You speak of Lord Byron and me. There is this great difference between us. He describes what he sees—I describe what I imagine. Mine is the hardest task.'

**E.** Why yes, because Keats's transcendence in *Endymion* of 'the light of common day' was a struggle—witness the many variants which the *apparatus criticus* records—but it made him a much greater poet than Byron. Transcendence without effort is rare. Shakespeare, Mozart, and possibly Catullus came nearest; which isn't to deny that some men have been able to polish second thoughts till they looked like spontaneity. With the aid of that discipline R. L. Stevenson became a great artist.

**AE.** Then you would say that art is posterior, not prior, to thought?

**E.** Posterior to everyday *Vorstellung*, yes; not to philosophical thought. Maybe it is a 'second negation', cancelling the prose of everyday and returning to an enriched initial innocence. Art is most assuredly rational, even if some artists have failed where Keats succeeded, failed to discipline a strong and passionate imagination——

**AE.** Dylan Thomas, for example.

**E.** And even if great art be near allied to madness.

**AE.** What about abstract art, and what about music?

**E.** To me abstract art which approaches total divorce from common experience is at best mere decoration. I don't know what criterion the artist is working with beyond 'first negation' of what went before, and that by itself can lead to nothing coherent. On the other hand, there must be an element of memory in any colour, shape, or sound that an artist can present, and it may be that sheer colour, shape, and sound are susceptible to more aesthetic development than I can sense. I still find it hard to believe (though I have tried) that abstract art has reached or can reach a very exalted level. In my sourer moods I say to myself, this is an *avant-garde* marching without map or compass in purely centrifugal directions.

I've heard you. What about music?

In music the whole range of human emotions is transcended, less articulately, though not less genuinely, than it is in poetry. It makes of them a mysterious untranslatable structure of its own. It is only loosely connected with other art forms in its development. How else could the truth, the *Wahrheit*, of Bach, Handel, Haydn, and the miracle of Mozart have co-existed with the dessicated falsity of eighteenth-century verse?

Not only with the verse. I once sat in the charming 'Little Theatre' at Munich listening to *Figaro*. I found the conjunction delightfully appropriate, but the kinship of the contemporary rococo *décor* with Mozart's music is extremely superficial.

Extremely, and one might wonder how Shostakovich managed to emerge, though it wasn't without difficulty, from the sterile tyranny of Soviet Russia. But we are wandering away from our subject.

As we generally do.

Let's get back to man as concrete universal. Even if it will be another meander, I shall indulge you by again talking about Shakespeare, because he is the nearest approach to the concrete universal in my experience. Aristotle justly says that the knowledge of contraries is the same, and I'd like to exhibit Shakespeare this time in the light of the misconceptions and abuses to which he has been intermittently subjected since 1660, when his plays were revived after the Puritan interlude.

The Restoration attitude was not, I take it, 'Others abide our question. Thou art free.'?

That was written during a nineteenth-century interval of comparative sanity. It wasn't true in the seventeenth and eighteenth centuries, and it's rapidly ceasing to be true now.

**AE.** What are the misconceptions?

**E.** The persistent misconception has been the belief that a great play of Shakespeare is not an individual unity in which Shakespeare's universality is manifestly concreted in each detail of characterization and language, but a theme which may be legitimately varied to suit the taste of each new age. The universality of Shakespeare is treated as an abstraction, a generality, which each generation may concrete as it pleases.

**AE.** That wouldn't have worried Shakespeare: he did that sort of thing himself. But he was obviously unaware of his own greatness, and that makes all the difference.

**E.** To understand what happened to Shakespeare after 1660 one has to remember that for well over a century, between *Samson Agonistes* and *Lyrical Ballads*, English poetry, bar bits of Burns from over the border, was virtually in suspended animation. It was frozen into smooth and shallow verse by a cold wind of neo-classicism from France; but it never achieved the icy splendour of Corneille, or the passion and subtlety of Racine's rhetoric, which can rise into poetry.

**AE.** Because it was English and not French?

**E.** Yes, the French genius was too different. There wasn't the nearness of French and English that there was in Chaucer's day. All we got from French drama was a pauperizing of our vocabulary in the interest of a quickly ossifying poetic diction, a mild respect for the unities, a tendency to substitute the type for the individual, a total artificiality in all forms of poetry, and that maddeningly pervasive habit of antithetical writing which still rigidified equally the verse and the prose compositions of Samuel Johnson.

**AE.** Who is only tolerable in the medium of Boswell. I agree strongly about the artificiality. Restoration and eighteenth-century poets writing about Nature stifle the mind. Thomson's *Seasons* and even Gray's *Elegy* make me think of the *immortelles* reposing glass-covered on the graves of Père Lachaise. But you must admit some robustness and snap in Dryden's verse. At least it's better than the miniature elegance of Pope. How did Pope dare to translate the *Iliad*?

That is the point I was coming to. The Resotration outlook, which took a long time to fade, was a narrow and very conceited one. In the specious present of their men of taste, the past, till one got back to Antiquity, was more a reject than a source of nourishment. They reacted to the Puritans with the bawdiest comedy, which Louis XIV would never have permitted.

Dear me, no. Molière never shocks. The bawdy plays were also due, I suppose, to the introduction of actresses who had no stage tradition, and to the encouragement of the Merry Monarch himself. I always think the busts and paintings of Charles II show a streak of meanness if you compare them with those of Louis XIV. *Le Roi Soleil* has an arrogant air, but he looks much more open and frank.

If you leave out the somewhat overrated Rabelais, the French have always been far better than we at managing the lower levels of sex with tact and wit. But it was not only the Puritans to whom the men of the Restoration felt themselves superior. They perhaps sensed a certain rude nobility in the Elizabethans, but they regarded them as crude and uncivilized compared with themselves.

And when they revived Shakespeare?

It was murder most foul, but sometimes quite funny; worth a meander.[1]

Let's have some fun.

The most ludicrous effort was probably a synthetic play by Sir William Davenant (who was, mark you, Poet Laureate), called *The Law against Lovers*. To brighten up black comedy he drops Beatrice and Benedick out of *Much Ado* into *Measure for Measure*. Benedick becomes Angelo's brother. After pleading in vain for Claudio's life he raises a rebellion in Vienna, and defeats Angelo in a battle off stage. In the end Isabella, though only after suggesting to Julietta that she shall substitute for her and go to bed with Angelo, marries Angelo, who really was only testing Isabella's virtue all the time. Chunks of the two plays are stuck

[1] Most of what follows I have gratefully pillaged from *Shakespeare Improved*, Hazeldon Spencer, Harvard University Press, 1927.

together with patches of dreary Davenant, who is constantly improving Shakespeare's lines to sheer flatness to make them clearer. In his version of *Macbeth* his deafness to the music of the spheres, which exceeds even his blindness to dramatic situation, is superbly illustrated in his change of 'After life's fitful fever he sleeps well.' It becomes, 'He after life's short fever sleeps. Well,/ Treason has done its worst', the 'Well' going with what follows. He also gives Lady Macduff a big part as a pillar of morality to counterpoise Lady Macbeth. In Act IV Macbeth wonders whether he really ought to go out and fight when his wife is so poorly. He wavers between love and honour, as if the two of them were Rodrigue and Chimène.

**AE.** Did nobody stop him?

**E.** Oh no, they liked it. He then collaborated in a massacre of the *Tempest* with Dryden, who in fact had considerable admiration for Shakespeare, and was now and again nearly a poet. Competent critics have praised his *Troilus and Cerssida*, though it preserves Cressida's virtue and ends with her suicide! But in *The Tempest* he fairly lets himself go, and he probably did most of the work. The cast is almost doubled, on the antithetical principle, with (*a*) an heir to the Dukedom of Mantua, whom Prospero has brought up from infancy in concealment, and who has never seen a woman; (*b*) sisters for Miranda and Caliban; finally (*c*) a spirit girl-friend for Ariel, who has been faithfully waiting fourteen years for his release. The chief purpose in this increase in the island's population is to have fun with the four innocents finding out the facts of life. Dryden being, as Spencer remarks, 'an absolute master of genteel smut', the dialogue becomes pretty fruity.

**AE.** Tut tut.

**E.** Among many outrages the crowning blasphemy was Nahum Tate's version of *Lear*, mangled and patched with the ghastliest doggerel. A love affair between Edgar and Cordelia, who is sometimes quite a little coy and calculating, runs through the play to a happy ending in which Edgar and Albany rescue Lear and Cordelia at the last moment. This muck—O horrible! O horrible! most horrible!—held the stage for a century and a half! Garrick played in it. It shocked Addison, but on the ground that the original is too terrible, and that innocence should be rewarded and not afflicted on the stage, it was approved by Dr. Johnson.

Who thereby damned himself for ever as a critic of Shakespeare. What do you suppose the acting was like from the Restoration onwards? Was it very ham?

I doubt it. The neo-classical tradition was against violence on the stage—not that the English took much account of that—and the refined elegance on which the age prided itself should not have encouraged ham acting. I fancy ham was the vice of the more romantic nineteenth century. I can remember in the beginning of the twentieth Frank Benson tending to rant and distort his words in a way you wouldn't hear nowadays, when mumbling is the common fault. Forbes Robertson and Matheson Lang were all right. I never saw Henry Irving, but both my parents regarded him as quite impossibly ham. As to the previous centuries, we have the well-known evidence of Fielding's *Tom Jones* that Garrick did not overact, and there is some evidence that Betterton, the most famous English actor of his time, who died in 1710, was carefully produced as Hamlet and Henry VIII by Davenant, who had seen those parts played by actors coached by Shakespeare himself. So we may hope that Betterton followed Hamlet's advice to the Players.

And the moderns?

The fashionable modern director just doesn't deserve Shakespeare any more than did his Restoration or eighteenth-century counterpart. The present age is neither elegant nor romantic but feebly permissive and—as the seventeenth and eighteenth centuries certainly were not—dully egalitarian. Our playwrights and scriptwriters mostly season a plotless and obscurely rambling matter with sex and violence as the commercial traveller in a cheap hotel pours Worcester Sauce on his tasteless food. The Shakespearian producer on the whole keeps the text and doesn't mess about with the structure very much, but he does his best to modernize, which means today to vulgarize. He tends to dress the play irrelevantly, eschewing doublet and hose, perhaps absurdly supposing that he thereby symbolizes

Shakespeare's universality; but sex and democracy are his guiding stars.

**AE.** Respect for the text we still owe to the great nineteenth-century advance (though I suppose Dr. Johnson must be given some credit) in Shakespeare scholarship and the prescribing of Shakespeare's plays for schoolboy study. A certain piety arose. The works of Shakespeare were allowed as well as the Bible in the cells of Her Majesty's prisons. Just as Restoration smut was a backlash after Cromwell and the Puritans, so our present peculiarly tasteless and humourless sexuality is, I suppose, still a reaction (How long, O Lord? How long?) from Bowdler and the Victorians.

**E.** Only the French, as I said, should be allowed to deal with sex in any artistic medium. Their post-Rabelaisian attitude to sex has always been intelligently adult and witty, and they still respect their own great literature. I went a year or two ago in London to a film of *Romeo and Juliet*. Shakespeare's lovers were aristocratic, and they are ill played by teenagers talking near-cockney who have learnt no elocution and no manners. Shakespeare spared his boy actors the cruder forms of caress. They were not cuddled. I left after the balcony scene, mentally puking. The Restoration was bawdy, but it had at least a pretence of gentility.

**AE.** I saw a snatch of a *Romeo and Juliet* film on TV. A monk cat-called as Juliet entered Friar Lawrence's cell.

**E.** As if it were *Till Death Us Do Part*. But it is sex as a complete perversion of Shakespeare's characterization which nauseates. I retched slightly at a well known director's asinine suggestion that Puck put an ass's head on Bottom because a donkey is notoriously a highly sexed animal, and I recently read a review of a production of *As You Like It* in which Rosalind and Celia start as Lesbians. That's not really the way I like it.

**AE.** Good God! I suppose the deserted Celia married Oliver out of pique. But what a fruitful prospect for that director! Helena and Hermia, for example:

> Two lovely berries moulded on one stem;
> So, with two seeming bodies, but one heart.

Beatrice and Hero had been bedfellows for a twelvemonth before the eve of that fatal wedding day. That was really why Beatrice commanded Benedick to kill Claudio.

Paulina had Hermione in purdah for sixteen years, and Antigonus had been conveniently eaten by a bear.

We're getting scurrilous; but seriously, with that sort of cheap and dirty stunt, the poetry evaporates, the air smells sour, and it has no connection whatever with Shakespeare.

It will go on so long as we continue to sink on the dreary mud-flats of multiform sexual promiscuity and unindividual egalitarianism, 'all life level'd down to where the lowest can reach'. I doubt if even the French could help us now. When you have abolished all the rules and respectabilities, there's nothing left to laugh at in any sexual situation. What an unsubtle race we are!

It must anyhow be admitted that from Davenant to Tate, and from Peter Brook onwards, the concrete universality of Shakespeare has not been greatly enhanced. Tomorrow we had better talk about something else.

Before we finish tonight, let's see what we've made of a man as concrete universal. We have tried to put together a singular organic body, much of which is in fact inanimate, with a mind which has developed both logically and temporally from sense to thought, progressively losing singularity as it puts on universality.

Itself becoming universal because what it thinks is universal, and achieving self-consciousness so far as it can unite what it sees of itself with what others see of it.

Inheriting the past but also contributing to it; giving itself and receiving itself in a diversity of human contexts—what a vast world of interconnection and overlap!—even, we dared to suggest, developing and manifesting itself beyond the death of its body; as perhaps most markedly in the western world did Plato, Aristotle, Jesus of Nazareth, and Shakespeare. If they had ceased at death to mould the minds of men, what an unthinkably different world ours would have been!

**E.** In all this a man's mind remains concretely universal, truly individual, save so far as its measure of inevitable finitude dilutes a man's thoughts towards mere generality and sense awareness, cabins and confines the fulfilling of his limitless desires, and to that extent ties him still to individuality by exclusion, and keeps him a man among other men.

**AE.** This is so difficult and so important that I'd like to try to put it in my own way, even if I only succeed in repeating you. If you put the initial emphasis on a man's finitude, you see him as an expanding world of experience, a world of divers activities and passivities. This world radiates from one among other singular originating centres, each of which has a name, a place, and a date of its own. A man is a little like a Leibnizian monad, though far from windowless, in that he mirrors and expresses the universe from his own point of view. From that private point of view he sees, if he reflects, his initial singularity bound up with his sentience, and rooted in yet more primitive levels of Nature. But with the very beginning of his ideal expansion the universal enters into his experience, and with the universal comes an ambivalence which you can only very clumsily untwist into two separate histories. You cannot even divide here cleanly and with confidence between temporal and logical process. The universal, however rudimentary its manifestation, betokens the immanence in a man of absolute spirit and the transcending of his finitude; but so far as his thought is merely general, and rests for support on images, so far his finitude remains, even if he has attained a degree of self-criticism which implies an inkling of the Absolute.

**E.** The ambivalence you speak of is once again the puzzle of finite and infinite. You can't untwist them into two separate histories: they are simply not separable. You still talk as if they merely confronted one another and had somehow got entangled; but if that were the case they would both be finite. I thought this really had become clear. The logic of the true and the spurious infinite is one of Hegel's most profound insights. We discussed it apropos of time and eternity; we meet it again in trying to relate man and absolute spirit, because it is an all-pervasive correlation. That is why Hegel makes it a very primitive category which all its successors sublate. I refuse to believe that the universe is in the last resort spuriously infinite, and I know no better refutation of the view than Hegel's.

Yes I see now. The finite-infinite tie appears at every level on the scale. A self-sufficient perfect God creating Nature and man by an arbitrary act of will—what Milton, for example, believed —becomes *eo ipso* finite. But the same unbreakable linkage appears at the very dawn of logic. How indeed should man escape it? Yet unless we opt for a pantheism in which the human person vanishes, there must be an appreciable and necessary distinction between finite and infinite though there can be no separation.

We agreed that the constituent phases of absolute spirit must be graded, variously real, approximations to itself. In other words the finite, thing or man, cannot be more than imperfectly individual, and to the extent of its imperfection it is individual by exclusion. So that it is by virtue of its imperfection that the finite is distinct from the infinite. Yet that is a *necessary* distinction. But don't think I underrate the difficulty of the problem. Any theory of this baffling ambiguity which we contrive will be the more obviously a product of overlapping ignorance and knowledge the more it enters into detail. Whichever we elect to talk of, the finite or the infinite, we cannot keep our tongues clear of the other.

On this large scale the problem is baffling, but there is surely help in the fact that within man himself one meets analogous ambiguity at every stage. We agreed yesterday that body and mind constitute a unity which somehow bestrides two distinguishable but inseparable levels of Being. It is all the same problem, totally insoluble if you try to juxtapose the two terms on the same level. You have made it perfectly clear that the Infinite juxtaposed to the finite becomes itself finite. Analogously, the human mind juxtaposed to the human body becomes itself physical and, to the cave-dwelling observer, identical with the brain. The body participates in the mind, which dominates it and expresses itself in and through the body. The body-mind unity is in fact a hierarchy of phases, such as life and sensibility, whose mutual relation is analogous. Science parted from Aristotle, who had more than an inkling of the difficulty, and it has since worked on the flat for its own perfectly legitimate and mainly practical purposes, abstracting wholly from value. But this problem science, observing through its intellectually egalitarian spectacles, cannot even fairly formulate. The detachable singular soul was at least a courageous if naïve solution, but Hegel's dialectic has been, since Aristotle, the only plausible attempt to bridge a gap which no amount of thinking on the flat could mend.

**E.** That, too, is not final, though I cannot see beyond it.

**AE.** But we can't give up. We must, as Aristotle bade us, be as immortal as we can.

# VI

## LEVELS OF SPIRIT

. Can we today examine the charge against Hegel of panlogism?

▸ I'd rather not—yet; though I admit it has got to be discussed.

▸ Well, can we get on to dialectic? Hegel's if you must, but you've been leaning pretty hard on Hegel, and you are supposed to be drafting your own philosophical testament. Do now try to come a bit cleaner on your own views.

▸ I do, as Paton accepted Kant, accept Hegel as my father Parmenides, though my acknowledgement of intellectual sonship is based on no feeling of racial affinity. Hegel bears no blame for Hohenzollern Germany or the Third Reich, but since well before 1914 I have felt myself, unlike most of my compatriots, far closer to the French than to the Germans. I have philosophical ancestors, too, a few of whom I should like to be thought to take after, however remotely. Furthermore a testament is a revocable document. You ask me to talk self-committally, but I confess that when I try to think, old as I am, I no more rule out the possibility of changing my mind than I take pains to avoid repeating myself. I'll talk about dialectic, or in that direction, if you like, and since I am to come clean, I'll tell you that the first stage in my coming to believe dialectic to be the proper method of philosophy was not so much my reflection on the way men think and argue; it was far more my impression that all great thinkers and, I believed, most thoughtful men have conceived the universe not only as a unity but as some sort of hierarchy, some kind of developing series of levels. Doubtless theism, and with it social hierarchy, have largely provided the basis of this *Weltanschauung*, but I have always believed that a deeper foundation underlay them.

▸ How did you go about looking for your deeper foundation?

**E.** I wanted to see hierarchy—I use the word broadly—established with its roots below the level of *explicit* value. I had no use for pious theology, but I was sure that a sound philosophy must find the supreme values, the eternal verities, ubiquitously immanent and implicit, though merely implicit, at levels where the unthinking man might only see indifference. Only so, I believed, if one rejected as I did intrinsic values in the shape of a personal Deity's imposed edicts, and death as a summons to Heaven or to Hell, could one escape a barren scepticism.

**AE.** Where did you first find what you wanted?

**E.** Always remembering that he was a Platonist, I found it first in the linked moments of Aristotle's system: matter and form, potential and actual, change and activity. I won't dwell on him at length here. I've done that in print, treating him both independently and in connection with Hegel.

**AE.** Without great effect, I fear. It's surprising how people can distort the plainest facts of a system when it has gone out of fashion.

**E.** Witness the relatively short chapter on Aristotle in Sir Karl Popper's *The Open Society and Its Enemies*, which might be described as 'infinite rubbish in a little room'. When a man tells you that the doctrine of the mean was a doctrine of compromise, and then chases an imaginary contradiction in Aristotle's theory of definition without ever asking himself what is the *definiendum* in question, he proves once more that, as John Webster remarked, detraction is the sworn friend to ignorance.

**AE.** Nor does he improve when he then turns to vilify Hegel.

**E.** No. I only want to make a point or two above Aristotle. His *Scala Naturae* is a developing series in which each term presupposes its predecessor but not its successor. In terms of matter and form this means that at every level above primary matter, which is only an ideal limit, the matter to be informed in order to constitute *that* level is always the already informed matter of the previous level. This implies—here is the point I want to stress—that you will not discover the essential nature of the real at a given level by merely analysing its proximate matter, the informed matter, that is, of which the prior stage consisted, and which has now become the matter, but not the form, of the given stage.

. An example would help a lot.

. Very well. This developing series gives us the structure of Aristotle's sublunary world, though above it the story is rather different. The plainest example of it is perhaps the three grades of ψυχή, 'life' or 'soul', which constitute form as specific activity and purpose in the animate world. The form of the plant is the twin functions of nutrition and reproduction. These, modified and developed, subserve the animal as its proximate matter, but the specific form which defines the animal is a new unity of sensation and appetition. Analogously, the informed matter of which the animal consists becomes the proximate matter of man, whose specific form is rational activity. Man eats and grows and reproduces his kind; man sensates and lusts; but in man these functions are modified and developed to subserve the fresh unity of reason. Man is no more the naked ape than he is the forked radish. Every stage differs at once in kind and degree from each of the others.

. And below plant life?

. There the scale descends in analogous grades through Aristotle's rudimentary physico-chemical world, down to the opposites, hot-cold, fluid-dry, which mate in pairs to become matter for the four elements. The obsolescence of Aristotle's natural science, or natural philosophy (in him they are barely parted), has left intact the genuinely philosophic principle of developing series, graded stratification. It is not expressly dialectical in Aristotle, but it clearly reaches forward to the principle which animates Hegel's philosophies of Nature and Spirit.

. In fact, as we implied yesterday, when we touched on the body-mind relation, genuine philosophy cannot in any age work on the flat. It must accept differences of level, degrees of truth and reality, as its normal field of inquiry.

. I'm sure of it. I see it everywhere, this linkage of levels. Think, for example, of the variety of levels at which sexual love may exist between two persons, even simultaneously as well as successively.

**AE.** 'Love', said F. H. Bradley, 'is a plant which has blossoms as well as roots in the earth. But remember, this is God's mystery.'[1]

**E.** Yet I think it is not a mystery without parallel, and I'd like here to make a point in parenthesis, which I ought perhaps to have made earlier. I said that each grade of Aristotle's ψυχή differed at once in kind and degree. I meant that human, animal, and plant soul are each a different species of ψυχή, but each also manifests 'soul' in a different degree. The three species are thus not co-ordinate but grades on a scale. But degree and kind are here so fused that the degree cannot be quantitatively measured. You can predicate higher or lower of these grades, but the absurdity becomes obvious if you attempt measurement. One can safely say that inseparability of degree and kind distinctively characterizes any philosophical scale of forms, any hierarchy philosophically viewed.

**AE.** Then if we say that absolute spirit constitutes itself in a series of self-approximations, we mean that so far as we are able to grasp these approximations philosophically, we must see them as differing in degree and kind inseparably; never the one difference without the other. That is just what differences of *Wahrheit* are. Where degree and kind fuse, there spirit is immanent, and that is what Hegel's dialectic is trying to express in every triad. Am I right?

**E.** You are, and when Robin Collingwood treated the whole subject of philosophical forms admirably in his *Philosophical Method*, he pointed out that in the field of natural science degree and kind fall apart. The natural scientist, working on the flat, *can* measure degree. In fact he spends much time in the laboratory doing just that. That is why it is so interesting to find the principle of developing series expounded with passion by a qualified physician who held successively chairs of physical chemistry and social studies. I mean Michael Polanyi. He was not brought up, I think, on Aristotle or idealist philosophy, but his position is in some respects strikingly close to both.

**AE.** You mean he reached hierarchy by a different route?

**E.** He saw the universe stratified more or less on that principle. He

[1] *Aphorism 75.*

points out[1] that the parts of a machine are amenable to physico-chemical analysis, and that their precise physico-chemical structure is not only the necessary condition of the machine's functioning, but also the level, the stratum, where you must look to find the fault if the machine breaks down. But no amount of physico-chemical analysis of these parts will enable you to understand the unity which comprehends them, namely the machine itself. That can only be understood in terms of the purpose which it serves, and the man to explain that is not the physical chemist but the engineer.

I. And I suppose you would say that, analogously, there is more in physics than its mathematical basis can explain. But all that is fairly obvious, isn't it?

I. Perhaps, but let me get on. Polanyi points out that this relation between the two levels holds equally if you substitute for the machine the living organism in so far as it functions mechanically, which in large measure it obviously does. You learn the truth of this, I may say, the moment you are taken seriously ill. Your doctor demands samples of your blood and urine. He takes your blood pressure and temperature and cardiographs your heart-beat. He then either turns you over to the surgeon or prescribes a drug or both. The whole of that diagnostic analysis (and synthesis) is conducted from the physico-chemical level. Of course your doctor and your surgeon must know what life itself is to the extent of recognizing the healthy or unhealthy functioning of your organism through sensible symptoms, and equally of course through the feel of life in themselves, that rudimentary self-consciousness through which we all know that we are alive and well or ill; but in contriving the means to health they are perpetually occupied at the lower level. They must know how to co-operate with the organism's tendency to self-regeneration, but all their techniques imply that they deal with organism only *qua* mechanism.

E. No doubt, but I see nothing so far that Aristotle or Hegel would have wanted to deny. Bosanquet said, 'Chemistry can say something of all material substances; but it can say less, in proportion, of those which have biological significance.'[2] That implies

---

[1] Cf. *The Study of Man*, Lecture II, Kegan Paul, 1959.
[2] *Philosophy and Science*, p. 238.

just the same point of view. What intrigues me is the location on the lower level of faults in the functioning of the organism, faults, Aristotle might have said, in its proximate matter. It is of course the only assumption on which the doctor can and does work effectively, unless he has in him a touch of the faith-healer or takes a tip from Coué. But those are not precise techniques, and he is likely to shy off them. The psychiatrist, too, is working on the lower level, whether he is trying to dig out a subconscious complex (which is faintly analogous, I suppose, to cutting out a carcinoma), or whether at a still lower level he uses drugs. But what I would like to know is how far can one extend this principle up the scale. Can one always in principle place the cause of human error and of human wickedness in all its shapes as a fault at a level lower than the explicit level of a man's activity?

**E.** An important and rather topical question. I feel sure that you are right in suggesting that the fault always occurs at the lower level, but I would remind you that the level from which you suggest extrapolating is little higher than that of mechanism, the level at which the healthy organism fulfils its purposive functions unconsciously, though not with precisely the sort of unconsciousness which characterizes the functioning of a motor-car or a computer.

**AE.** The difference which made Aristotle distinguish the product of an unconsciously teleological Nature from a human artifact?

**E.** Yes, but whatever you may think about unconscious teleology, be sure of this. So soon as we build up the hierarchy above mechanism, the relation between the two levels, between the specific form and the proximate matter, changes significantly in kind as well as degree. I thought you were hinting at a possible evasion of moral responsibility on these lines: The commonest cause of disease is the malfunctioning of a man's lower level where it is not in his control. So belike his robberies and his rapes, which surely in some way betoken disease, his black-mailings and his murders, were none of them his fault but all due to undetected trouble below the surface. So cowardice, dis-honesty, treachery, and brutality, as terms of reproach, fade away as the all-binding frost of determinism sets in. This is happening all over the place today both in theory and practice.

. The answer?

. Not, I think, to attack determinism with Goedel's theorem, but to point out that in man self-consciousness has developed a good deal beyond mere life. The moral life is a man's fashioning of himself in a social context out of his proximate matter, and the higher levels of his proximate matter are unlike the unconscious layers of bio-chemism, mechanism, and the teleological reciprocation of organs, because they are *selves*. He must, and he can, saving madness, dominate and shape to their proper rational uses his appetitive and aggressive selves, just because they are selves and not external forces. If faults arise in them they are in the main *his* faults. A drug may in some cases help from below, but he cannot disclaim responsibility. If he does, a fair reply would be, 'If this body isn't you, you won't mind if we hang it or put it in prison?' From Plato and Aristotle onwards, every sane moralist who has managed to steer between hedonism and puritanism has held some version of this view. It implies a relation between these levels of selfhood which is too subtle for precise formulation. It rejects determinism for self-determination, but it precludes the notion that a man's responsibility, or the claim of morality itself, can be absolute. The freedom which it offers is partial. It is an internal achievement which rests less on the power of choice than on what a man, given his heredity and social environment, has been able to make of himself, and for that reason it cannot exclude a residue of contingency. This view, however, reflects what decent people have always half instinctively accepted.

. Thank you. I am afraid, though, I have made you meander.

. Where were we? . . . Yes, I was saying in effect that doctors *qua* healers are bound to treat the organism as no more than mechanical or near-mechanical. I suspect that the biologists are in the same position. The geneticist studies (since Mendel with striking success) the mechanisms by which life is transmitted from individual to individual. The phylogenist investigates species evolving without conscious purpose, and without, it would seem, much unconscious purpose beyond a blind nisus towards survival and self-maintenance. What does he really mean by 'natural selection'? They are all really saying, aren't they, that you can't predict or control the behaviour of a living organism or a group of living organisms save in so far as you treat it as a machine? Kant's tortuous argumentation in the *Critique of Judgement* seems to end up more or less by justifying this attitude as assumed by the biologist: Although you can't make sense of Nature without assuming design, and although this assumption has a heuristic value for a biologist seeking mechanical connections, yet you mustn't suppose for a moment that this gives you and him any right to assert objective finality in Nature.

**AE.** And the experimental psychologist who studies the behaviour of rats in a maze?

**E.** He regards them, I imagine, as mechanisms which are to some extent self-adjusting under stimulus.

**AE.** What puzzles me is this. It is obvious that organisms are not mere mechanisms, and that no physico- or bio-chemical analysis can reveal their real nature, yet Polanyi and a few vitalists have been just voices in the wilderness to which the scientists turn a deaf ear. And it isn't only the natural scientists. The statistical methods of the sociologists, inheriting ultimately, I suppose, from Comte, suggest the same fallacy, namely that the parts in abstraction can tell you what the whole is.

**E.** Nevertheless the cloud of witness from science is too thick to puff away. Can you wonder that I used to accept the Crocean view that the special sciences are purely practical, purely economic in Croce's sense of the word, and are quite unconcerned with theoretical truth? I believed they didn't aim at discovering what the whole is, but only what facilities it offers for action, and for that good reason confined themselves to the lower levels. The present pharmacological phase of medicine rather encourages that view.

**AE.** Do you in fact now accept it?

**E.** Only in part. I think pure science and even pure mathematics are much closer to practical application than is believed by some scientists who wish to uphold the dignity of their profession and would rather not be thought of as technologists. The notion that science is advancing towards a glorious millenium when it will teach us the truth of all that really matters is to my mind simply absurd, because science is not equipped to move a step in that direction. All the same I cannot with Croce abandon the notion of a graded Nature, and natural science, despite its preference for moving on the flat, has done much to articulate its grades.

. I'm not sure that science hasn't done that by retreating step by step from Aristotle's teleological *Stufenleiter* of Nature.

. Rather more than that. Look at the multiplicity of simpler elements to which scientific analysis is continually reducing Aristotle's comfortably common-sense scale of earth, water, air, and fire. It's been a fascinating hunt for the ultimate atom, and I suppose one shouldn't be surprised when Russell tries to analyse mind on this same assumption that the real is everywhere the aggregation of simples. How should he see that spirit is that by which a whole surpasses the sum of its parts?

. How should he? But can we now climb your ladder a little higher? I was intrigued by your suggestion, though I think you had made it before, that life is a rudimentary self-consciousness. I suppose you wouldn't extend that to include liver-flukes and fungi?

. I was thinking of human life, but at every level the whole explains the parts, the developed the undeveloped, and not vice versa. That is the position we have just been defending, and have in fact been defending since we started to talk. I don't suggest that liver-flukes and fungi are self-conscious, but we have agreed that absolute spirit must constitute itself of graded approximations to itself, and I think one must try to grade consciousness and life—everything animate—in terms of approximation to self-consciousness. If you find liver-flukes and fungi too lowly, there is, I fear, no limbo outside an absolute whole to which they can be banished. The Absolute has got to contain not only these multifarious life-forms, but also the inanimate on earth and through the cosmos, to say nothing of the evil and error which beset human beings. Remember for your comfort that low degrees of *Wahrheit* are such *qua* the object of inadequate human apprehension as well as through the 'impotence' of Nature. Human minds have in them still a

measure of the self-externality and concomitant defects of levels
below them, as we saw just now. Yet Nature and the inanimate
only *are* as the objective 'other' of mind, which you and I are
seldom able to grasp as more than human minds.

**AE.** Then perhaps I was right in interpreting Hegel's saying that the
*an sich* of the world below consciousness is only *für uns* to mean
not merely that we know that world whereas it doesn't know
itself, but that its Being is the inseparable 'other' of our consciousness, and is therethrough known to absolute spirit.[1] We
agreed the other day to a provisional verdict of 'not proven',
but I think you have come round to the view I suggested.

**E.** I think perhaps I evaded the issue because that position is so
hard to state without making it sound like subjective idealism.
But I will try again. I am sure that the notion of an inanimate
thing subsisting except as an 'other' of thought does not stand
up to careful criticism. Its independent subsistence, which in
everyday life we accept and must accept without question, is a
status accorded by thought, and it is valid only within thought.
It signifies an *alienated* 'other', but the alienation is still a difference within the identity of thought and Being.

**AE.** You mean it is the self-alienation of absolute spirit immanent
and self-constituting in the human mind; that to assume it to
be an absolute difference without identity may be a *sine qua non*
for practical common sense, but is nonsense if erected into
pseudo-philosophical realism?

**E.** I mean just that. Berkeley was on the right track, but he stopped
half-way and tried to lay too heavy a burden on God. To make
the *esse* of a perceived thing merely *percipi* by men *singillatim* or
even archetypally by God is to destroy its objective Being. The
same is true if you make the *esse* of what is thought simply
*intelligi*. Berkeley made the same mistake as Spinoza in a more
elementary way. The unity of thought and Being doesn't
abolish objective Being, it constitutes it.

**AE.** Good. Before we go back to life and self-consciousness, there is
one point which ought to be stated clearly. You said, if I understood you, that a sound philosophy must envisage the intrinsic

---

[1] See p. 40, above.

values as immanent, though only implicit, at the lowest level of Being.

. Certainly. Philosophy, in contrast to science, is never value-free. But as the scale descends, value is too merely implicit, too merely privative, as Aristotle called the negative aspect of matter, to allow differentiation of one value from another.

. That suggests to me—no, it makes me perfectly certain—that your immanent criterion of intrinsic value is in effect true individuality, the concrete universal, and that you equate the merely implicit presence and privation of value with dispersedness, self-externality?

. Right again. In that Bosanquet helped me towards Hegel.

. Then *das Wahre*, like Plato's ἀληθές, becomes the good as well as, or rather in one with, the true and the real. The notion that human intrinsic values are purely subjective would seem to you false, and its extreme form in the shape of emotivism, which transfers them from reason to feeling, grossly false?

. Barbarous.

. Your belief in the ubiquitous immanence of value must considerably affect your conception of what thought is.

. Assuredly. That is implied in the conception of *Wahrheit* which we have now reached. But I should like to postpone direct discussion of it for the moment.

. All right. For the moment life and self-consciousness again.

. Hegel treats life in various contexts, even making Life a category of the Idea, because he sees in it an advance on mechanism and teleology. I often find him hard to follow, but I will start with the notion, which he accepts, of organism as constituted of organs which are reciprocally means and ends to one another. One might, perhaps, looking back to the lower level, call it a machine with a certain capacity for self-regeneration. But the living organism is more than the sum of its parts, even when they are conceived teleologically as in reciprocal service to one another. There is no life apart from organisms, yet life is not localized in the organism. One might say that its sovereignty is omnipresent, but it would be truer to say that life, being the herald of spirit, contains the organism as its proximate matter, transcending it, cancelling its self-externality, and emerging as its immaterial unity, which is the truth of it.

**AE.** A union of two levels by transcendence, baffling to the flat-minded natural scientist and only intelligible within the assumption of absolute spirit as immanent and active in the transcendence. That in religious *Vorstellung* would, I suppose, be the grace of God.

**E.** Unless you make some such assumption, you must either deny difference of level, or you must accept it positivistically as a fact for which you have no explanation to offer and no intention of looking for one.

**AE.** And either is a lapse to the unexamined life which is not, says Plato, to be lived by a man. But what about self-consciousness?

**E.** The vast diversity of shapes which life can assume should be a warning that no *Stufenleiter*, no developing series of levels which we construct, can claim precision, especially where we are trying to deal with spirit's first self-manifestation as the truth of Nature. I presume a fungus doesn't feel, but in man life *is* a feeling, unless he has sunk in sleep or coma to a vegetable level. I am not sure whether I can distinguish the feeling of life in me as the prius of all my specific feelings, or whether it is simply a sense of existence given me in coenaesthesis, but in either case it is immediate feeling. At this stage it can hardly be described save as the potentiality of what will emerge as a self aware at once of itself and of its 'other', of its object-world, that is, which it will then distinguish from itself. The two sides or moments of this awareness can't be separated, and this 'other' is ultimately an other self. So I feel justified in regarding this emergence from the life-feeling—or better this transcendence of the feeling of life—as the genesis of self-consciousness, and consequently in calling the feeling of life the germ of self-consciousness.

**AE.** Very well; so far as it goes I accept that; but all you have shown me is a transcendence of life straight into the initial phase of cognition. Surely there are intermediate levels even if one cannot establish them precisely. If, for instance, you were to consult

Hegel's *Philosophy of Spirit*, you would be told that attention produces out of feeling a spatio-temporal intuition, which already unites a rudimentary subject with the objective this-here-and-now from which it distinguishes itself. This rises into *Vorstellung*, 'pictorial thinking', or, perhaps better at this stage, merely 'presentation'.[1] *Vorstellung* begins with memory in the form of recollection, *Erinnerung*, the 'inwardizing' which overcomes self-externality. Recollection 'takes up the intuition', says Hegel, 'into the universality of the *ego*'. There it becomes an image, and when a fresh intuition turns up and is recognized as identical in content with the first intuition now become image, the latter has become the formal universal under which the new intuition is subsumed. The image now approximates more and more nearly to the true universal of thought. It is first a symbol representing something which is different from itself but yet akin to itself, as the eagle was the symbol representing the strength of Jove.

. Yes. I don't know whether that sort of symbolism really represents a necessary stage in the development of thought. I seem to remember Berkeley and Hume trying to explain universality by saying that somehow the singular idea comes to symbolize and stand for all the other ideas of its kind. They don't tell us how.

. Hegel puts it in as a level leading beyond hieroglyphs to linguistic symbols as arbitrary signs. We thus reach language, without which thought is not possible, and the moment of memory, which Hegel calls the mechanism of intelligence, now emerges as mechanical verbal memory, which demands no attention from the speaker and leaves him time to think.

. Thank you for filling in. I admit the gap, but you never give me time. On the whole I think Hegel's construction of stages in the development of human thought is still better than that of most subsequent psychologists, and they, envisaging no operative over-all universe, have not done much to explain how the stages connect. Hegel himself thought Aristotle's *De Anima* was better than anything written since, and I suspect he was right. Any further comment?

[1] See Hegel, *Encyclopaedia*, §§446 ff.

**AE.** Yes. Besides leaping rather hastily from the feeling of life to the beginning of cognition, you have so far said nothing of any development of feeling into volition. There must be some sort of bifurcation between thought and will even if it is only another distinction of inseparables. Lastly I am curious to hear what you propose to do about the development of feeling into emotion. You denounced emotivism rather curtly, but I shouldn't suspect you of wanting to substitute a purely intellectualist theory of intrinsic values. Hegel said that nothing great in the world is achieved without passion, and by passion he meant the canalization of all emotional urge in one direction. He had world-history in mind when he said it, but the *Phänomenologie* strongly suggests that he believed passion to be a condition of great thought as well as of great deeds.

 **E.** And of great art. Incidentally, in paraphrasing Hegel's *Philosophy of Spirit* you failed to mention that recollection, *Erinnerung*, leads not only to reproductive *Vorstellung* and therethrough to cognition but also to the free productive imagination, *Phantasie*, of the artist and of the religious man who finds truth in the form of allegory and myth. I would also point out that the portion of the *Philosophy of Spirit* which you considerably abridged falls under the heading of *Geist* and under the subheading *Subjective Geist*. *Geist* is perhaps here better translated as 'mind' rather than 'spirit'. It is preceded by a section on consciousness and, before that, one on soul, *Seele*, which is here more or less equivalent to 'life', because Hegel is elaborating Aristotle's ψυχή, not the Christian immortal soul. In those two sections of the developing series first life and then consciousness gradually emerge from Nature as its truth, and as yet there is no bifurcation of theoretical and practical, thought and will.

**AE.** How then does the bifurcation come?

 **E.** It springs from the nature of self-consciousness. The object of consciousness, Hegel explains,[1] is the natural soul, but mind (sc. as self-consciousness) makes consciousness its object. It then finds itself producing within itself objects which belong to it as its own, but yet are implicitly existent on *their* own. It must

---

[1] Cf. ibid., §443 and *Zusatz*.

overcome their mere givenness, their presence as merely pre-supposed; it must really own them. This is cognitive, theoretical activity. But theoretical activity is subjective and one-sided. Mind must conversely free itself from this sheer subjectivity and objectify practically its aims and interests. The section you abbreviated was purely cognitive and subjective, and it is seen by Hegel as the necessary *prius* of the practical. It is from cognition that the will develops, but cognition and volition are inseparable in their distinction: thinking is willed activity, and will is intelligent. Will becomes its essentially free self only by giving itself a content in and through thought. It begins as immediate feeling, as an initial singularity which is no more than caprice (*Willkür*) seeking satisfaction in a miscellany of incompatible desires; but it develops itself from this into a con-cretely universal, truly individual, world. Mind in which cogni-tion and volition, the theoretical and the practical, are thus united is essentially free (self-determining) mind. It develops its objective world in the phases of Law (*Recht*), the morality of the individual conscience, and then the ethical institutions, the family, civil society, and the state.

Must we go into all that now? I want to know——

Yes we must. I want you to see in outline how powerfully Hegel builds up the ascent of the finite towards the infinite which it presupposes. Objective spirit, thus already manifest far beyond singular individuals, closes with, first, the interrelation of nation-states in international law, then with world-history, which is spirit as the dialectic of national civilizations succeeding one another in time. Subjective and objective spirit unite in absolute spirit, and we reach the final triad—art, religion, philosophy.

Yes I do see, but I want to know what place you and/or Hegel think feeling as emotion retains in this development, especially since you have rejected emotivism with scorn, located intrinsic value ubiquitously in the universe, and accepted the good as an aspect of *das Wahre*.

I had meant to try to move on from *Stufenleiter*, levels of deve-lopedness to dialectic, but if you want to talk about feeling and emotion we had better postpone that till tomorrow. You ask a difficult question, and I am not perfectly sure of the answer.

We decided the day before yesterday, when we were discussing crowds, that no emotion could consist of feeling quite devoid of logos, judgement. An emotion must be about something, however merely psycho-physical and confused the experience may be. Hegel's contribution to the subject is worth study, but I don't know whether it is fully acceptable.

**AE.** Let's have it anyhow.

**E.** To begin with I must cast back, and you must be patient. Your extract from the *Philosophy of Spirit* took us to the first phase of cognition, which is *Verstand*, understanding, not yet *Vernunft*, reason. *Verstand* is the element of thought in 'pictorial thinking' (*Vorstellung* in the broad sense). It is everyday common-sense thinking, which is refined, purged as far as possible of imagery, as the thinking of the special sciences. In science it is the explicit effort to extract and sever the universal essences taken to underly groups of sensible singulars and to detect affinities and necessary connections between them. These empirical universals are still a plurality, as are the sensible singulars from which they are extracted. Being a phase of theoretical mind, *Verstand* is subjective, and its objects assert their independence of it. Correspondingly, it takes itself, so far as it is embryonically self-conscious, for no more than a singular subject of experience, possessed of several more or less separate and mutually independent faculties, and experiencing among a plurality of similar separate singular experients. Its discursive movement through judgement and syllogism foreshadows rational thinking, but its object-world is severed from it and independent of it, and the content of its thinking, as I said, is universals (are they subjective or objective? The centuries have failed to decide), universals which are only a plurality of general characters individualized only in singular instantiation. In this world of severance and externality the merely linear inferences of the understanding can only start with borrowed premises, propositions merely presupposed, whether conclusions of similar inferences or taken up empirically.

**AE.** That was Hegel's charge against Descartes when he went beyond the *Cogito*, and against Spinoza when he failed to conceive his absolute substance as developing and adopted the geometrical method.

, Yes; those were lapses from reason to understanding. The inferences of the understanding are linear. They start always with a borrowed premiss which does not return upon itself. There is a factor of contingency, and the necessity in their conclusions is always hypothetical, *a tergo*, and mechanical, not a free self-determining. It is to escape the unease of this insecure hypothetical world that scientists, and even more often mathematicians, sometimes in their craving for certainty follow Aristotle and Descartes in postulating immediate self-evident intuition. You will remember what we said of Russell and his friends three days ago. On the other hand, understanding is a necessary phase or level on the way to rational thinking, a moment sublated, cancelled but preserved, in reason. Its rigid, one-sided abstractions *are* first negations which determine. Without it there would be no determinate characterization of anything.[1]

, So far as individuality rests on exclusion, understanding is responsible?

, Yes, and that just precisely shows its one-sidedness. To take it for the full nature of reason is disastrous.

, It is quite clearly alien to feeling. What about reason and feeling?

, The relation of emotion to higher levels of spirit is discussed by Hegel chiefly in connection with ethics and religion, as, for example, in *Encyclopaedia*, §471. Against the sentimentalists who exalt the heart at the expense of the head, he argues that good (meaning morally sound) practical feeling (which Wallace aptly renders as 'instinct of action') has an implicitly universal content which can be matured to rational form, and thereby explicitly grasped as necessary and universal. Reason is its true form. As mere immediate feeling it is singular and subjective, self-will rather than free will. Despite its implicit rationality it may become perverted and bad. As against the understanding and its one-sided abstractions, however, this emotional content may just possibly on occasion be the genuine totality. 'The difficulty for the understanding', says Hegel, 'is to free itself from the severance which it has arbitrarily imposed between the

[1] Cf. ibid., §467, *Zusatz*.

several faculties of feeling and thinking mind, and to come to see that in man there is only *one* reason in feeling, volition, and thought'. That disposes of the emotivists, who identify reason with the thought which the understanding severs completely from feeling. The seat of value thus becomes for them the abode of unreason.

**AE.** That, I agree, settles the emotivists. I suppose F. H. Bradley set an Absolute of sentience above his 'intellectual middle-space', which is in effect not much above the thinking of the understanding, because he could not accept Hegel's notion of reason and dialectic. If, on the other hand, we substitute dialectical reason for the thought of the understanding, can it be shown that value is inherent in the dialectic, and that all is gained and nothing lost in the development of the heart into the head, of the emotional content, that is, into rational thinking and knowing?

**E.** It is vital for Hegel to do that, but I confess that I'm not sure whether he succeeds. However, we've agreed to talk about dialectic tomorrow. Let's try to deal with the problem then.

# VII

## TRANSITION TO DIALECTIC

I know you are determined not to get tangled up in the detail of
the dialectic, but before we start talking about it on a larger
scale I would like to get clear the difference in principle between
the Hegelian dialectic and a *Stufenleiter* or developing series such
as we have in Aristotle's grades of ψυχή, and for that matter in
his grading of inanimate Nature below them. His *Scala Universi*
—I suppose that's what one might call it—has already risen
above the flat classification with which the understanding
works. The philosophic fusion of difference of kind with difference of degree is established, and with it surely sublation. Is
not plant soul *aufgehoben*, cancelled but preserved, in animal
soul? The dialectic is vastly more detailed and systematic, but
is there really any great difference in principle?

What you say is halfway to the truth. Aristotle had a shrewder
insight into human nature than most of his successors; and why
not? He could communicate with his fellows just as well as you
or I, and their average intelligence was extremely high. Doubtless above and below man his scale has become obsolete, yet his
*Stufenleiter* was a rational philosophic construction. One might
say that Hegel's dialectic was the result of trying to bridge the
gaps left by Aristotle, and I'm sure Hegel would have agreed.
But there remains one great difference. Aristotle's scale symbolizes the one-way urge in all things to imitate the divine, but it
does not imply the immanence of the divine in all things.
Aristotle places us midway on his scale, yet it remains a schema
which we contemplate rather than a universe moved—and we
with it—at once and in one by inspiration and aspiration.
Aristotle's νοῦς is one with its incomposite object in actual
knowing, but it is an intuition of the self-evident which is as
fully independent of the truths which follow from it by one-way
necessitation as is Aristotle's God independent of the world

which strives to imitate his pure self-concentrated activity. The world is not the other self of God, and thought, save in its isolated intuitions, does not find itself in its object. When these severances are mended, thought and Being reveal their unity through difference. That is the ideal of dialectic: every triad is to sever and mend the severance.

**AE.** So the static *Stufenleiter* is animated and transcended into dialectical movement?

**E.** Yes, but don't think of it as a transition from rest to movement. It is the *timeless* activity of spirit, the *eternal* severance and return of spirit upon itself which Hegel sees immanent and operant in the structure of every triad. That is why Marx's 'dialectical materialism' was a contradiction in terms and a perspicuous exhibition of error perverting truth. He took the dialectic as a straight line instead of a circle, and then turned it upside down.

**AE.** No doubt, but surely Hegel trying thus to present the universe *sub specie aeternitatis* is limited and finited by the epoch in which he lived? he admits it himself.

**E.** Oh yes. The dialectic is rational. Its reasoning is categorical, not hypothetical like the inferences of the understanding, because it borrows no premiss and rests on no presupposition. But its independence of presupposition doesn't make it perfect. It is still, as you say, the product of its epoch.

**AE.** Assuming that we are now a little clearer as to the nature of dialectic, could we pause before we plunge deeper? Could we first tackle my two problems of yesterday, the ubiquitous inherence of intrinsic value, and what I called the development of the heart into the head? They still puzzle me, and I don't think they are irrelevant to the question of dialectic.

**E.** I find the first the easier of the two. I see no difficulty in equating degree of intrinsic value with degree of concrete individuality in man, and even in Nature. The writer of *Genesis*, if I may copy Hegel and borrow from religious myth, says that after six days of creation God saw everything he had made, and, behold, it was very good. I think that, *mutatis mutandis*, that wasn't far wrong. Where intrinsic value could come from if it were not ubiquitously immanent, I can't think. And unless value is everywhere inherent, I don't see how evil and error, which have no original content of their own, could play their parasitic part as perversion of the good and the true. The nature of intrinsic value is reflected in the dialectical triad, which is always in some degree the universal concrescent in the individual. Have you a better definition of intrinsic value?

No, though what we know of the cosmos beyond the earth does not suggest a high degree of intrinsic value, whatever Jehovah may have thought of it. Value as individuality would in your view be the generic character of all intrinsic values, whereas truth, beauty, morality, or however you like to distinguish them, would be species of this generic character differentiating it in degree and kind in accordance with different moments of human nature?

In human life distinct but all-pervasive overlapping moments; and just because they do overlap, the claims and counter-claims of knowledge, art, morality, and religion, if you reckon it separate from morality, have throughout the history of civilization set men quarrelling on the larger issues, to say nothing of their more domestic but far bitterer strife within the field of each intrinsic value. I agree with you that values ought to form a philosophical scale, but I find the question extremely difficult.

Well let's see whether the heart and head problem can help us. I suspect that it will lead us back to the value-scale.

There the first, though now obvious, point of importance is that the thinking into which Hegel encourages a man to develop his emotional content is rational. It is not the cold, aseptic thought of the understanding, the sharply determinant first negation, but the result which contains its own process, the feeling which has returned upon itself as concrete thought. He is not telling a man to cut out the sentiment and face hard facts, but trying to persuade him that by thinking he can reach much solider ground for what might be called his value-beliefs. That would apply, I suppose, equally to the good-hearted sentimentalist who ought to become conscious of himself as a citizen with rights and duties to be intelligently exercised, and to the naïve religious devotee, who would do well to think about God rather more intelligently. The latter case reminds one that Hegel sees the final sublation of spirit through art and religion to philosophy as calm development rather than passage through contradiction. The content is throughout rational, and the dialectical movement is only a change of form from sense in art through imagination in religion to thought in philosophy. I think he should have made it equally a change of content. It was surely a development in kind as well as degree.

**AE.** It should on your account have been a development in kind and degree of individuality.

**E.** How would that work?

**AE.** I don't know. It's only just occurred to me . . . The work of art intensely individual, genuinely concrete universal, but because the form is sensuous, inevitably one among many. As against art, philosophy would be the effort to grasp all reality in thought as the concretely universal One.

**E.** And religion?

**AE.** Possibly the imitation of Christ as the perfect human individual.

**E.** Ingenious, and perhaps not without truth. But I doubt if it is Hegelian. Hegel seems always to think of religion much less as a practical way of life than as theology in mythical shape approximating to metaphysics.

**AE.** But at any rate in the moral sphere Hegel would have regarded the development as one in which form and content are inseparable?

**E.** I think so.

**AE.** Could we say, then, that in the moral sphere the passage from feeling to thought works like this: in the first negation the felt content is determined by, or as, its opposite, namely the thought of the understanding, and in the result, the complete triad, the content as felt and the content as understanding become a unity in which they are not merely inseparable but no longer distinct? Is that what reason, anyhow practical reason, really is for Hegel? Did Kant stop half-way in what must be a dialectical movement? Did he, I mean, stick in the antithetic phase, mistaking understanding for reason, and proclaim an irreconcilable opposition between reason and inclination?

I think he did, but I fancy there was a touch of unsublimated puritan feeling there as well, and that it wasn't a purely intellectual error. I think you are on the right track, but we must try now to get our minds clear about feeling and thought, which is what really irks you.

It is.

We said yesterday that life emerges as the immaterial unity of the organism, and that in man it emerges as feeling, in which at this stage the distinction of matter and form is quite latent; although what is there is not sheer matter, because if form is totally absent matter vanishes too.

As Aristotle showed?

Yes. Man, whom at this stage we might reasonably exemplify as the newborn babe, simply *is* this feeling, which would seem to lack all difference except, as the crying babe forces us to admit, that of pleasure and pain. But we too easily forget that from this barely determinate feeling develop *all* shapes of human experience. It is their only natural source. We agreed that a man goes whole into all his thoughts, acts, and passions, and this is the genetic aspect of the matter. Indubitably feeling developed to emotion can appear very sharply distinct from thought. It can deceive us into imagining it as something *sui generis*, a positive and independent force which can conflict with reason, destroy or pervert it. This especially seems so when violence rises from the psycho-physical level to accompany it. Yet we often praise an emotion because it seems to be in harmony with reason. It surely follows that in either case there must be some thought in the emotion.

So that neither a crowd nor a newborn baby can express absolutely blind feeling?

No. Aristotle tells us that there must be some logos informing the feeling to make an emotion,[1] and Hegel reminds us that 'there is only one reason in feeling, volition, and thought.'[2]

Two points. When you say that barely determinate feeling is the only *natural* source of human experience in all its shapes you are abstracting from the immanence of absolute spirit?

[1] See pp. 59–60, above.   [2] See p. 112, above.

**E.** Yes and no. Nature means nothing apart from spirit, and the immanence of spirit is at once implied if one talks of 'foreshadowing' or 'prefiguring.'

**AE.** Secondly, if there is thought in the emotion which conflicts with reason, is there, correspondingly, feeling in the reason which clashes with the emotion?

**E.** There must be. I don't see how you could have a genuine conflict either between two men or inside one man without feeling as well as thought on both sides. Reason alone, on the other hand, can provide the criterion for solving such a conflict.

**AE.** Reason with feeling in it?

**E.** Yes but reason with feeling in it sublated. There is thought in the emotion with which reason has clashed, but reason is the higher form and must in principle dominate.

**AE.** Then whereas understanding only determines feeling as its first negation, reason fully sublates it? That is rationalism as opposed to intellectualism?

**E.** Yes I think so; but we mustn't make too sharp a distinction between understanding and reason or we shall be in danger of making them separate faculties, which would bar the sublation of understanding by reason. Incidentally I ought perhaps to apologize for using 'understanding' and 'understand' in the ordinary English sense while at the same time using 'understanding' to translate *Verstand*, but I cannot find an alternative, and the same difficulty arises in German.

**AE.** Never mind. I don't think you have misled me. You've not, however, yet fully answered my question, but let's work our way with an eye on Hegel. Clearly when reason sublates feeling we reach the level of intrinsic value. It would seem natural to say that in art and religion anyhow reason has emotion sublated in it and pretty conspicuously preserved; but I find it confusing when Hegel apparently reverses the terms and makes reason the constant content and first of all sense, then imagination, and then thought, the form. It looks like some sort of jugglery.

**E.** I don't think so. You are forgetting that in philosophy form and content are one, mutually pervasive. If reason is constant in the development from art through religion to philosophy, it is reason as rational content, not reason metamorphosed by jugglery out of form into content. Correspondingly, sense, imagination, and thought, though without content they are nothing, here appear as the moment of form. In Hegel's conception of form and content there is a kind of duality on both sides of the distinction.

Much the same as the mutual self-constituting of finite and infinite?

I think so, but I'm sure we shall come back to Hegel's final triad again. Meanwhile let's try to finish off this problem about feeling in the higher forms of spirit. In morality, art, and religion there is quite indisputably feeling as emotion. Philosophy remains, and in human philosophizing I would say there certainly is emotion.

Would Hegel agree?

He ought to, though he does sometimes tend to shut his eyes to the extent of human finitude and ignorance. Yet he derides the notion that man can think without words. If language adheres to human reason, both as an indispensable support and a sign that man can only approximate to absolute spirit, why shouldn't that be true of emotion, too?

You are really saying that even at the top, even in philosophy, there is an analogy with pictorial thinking in which thought strives to supersede sense but is still indispensably supported by it?

Yes.

I agree with you, and I think we might here take a leaf out of Aristotle's book. Feeling is always pleasure or pain (a fact which I suggest supports your view of the ubiquity of value), and Aristotle holds that pleasure inseparably accompanies any unhindered activity and takes its character from the activity. He maintains this to be true not only of human activities but also of the eternal activity of God. So he would not have denied its specific feeling of pleasure to human philosophizing.

**E.** Nor, I suppose, its specific pain when it is frustrated. Plato, on the other hand, didn't attribute pleasure to God: he thought it *infra dig.* Hegel may have felt like that, too.

**AE.** Well, let's enjoy our philosophizing. You might now tell me your reaction to Hegel's dialectic, not triad by triad but in a more general form. What about Nature, for example?

**E.** Allowing for the fact that science progresses rapidly, and that Hegel inevitably can only try to interpret the science of his own day, and for the further fact of my own minimal knowledge of science, the dialectic of Nature seems to me to be tolerably sound. At any rate I feel sure that the ascent from sheer spatio-temporal self-externality must be the theme of a philosophy of Nature, though the mere fact that science develops is enough to show that no dialectic of Nature can be more than a rather sketchy interim report. I find the transition from the natural to the explicitly spiritual, and the ascent from sense to thought, which we have touched upon but inevitably telescoped, uniquely brilliant both in the *Phänomenologie* and in the more controlled *Philosophy of Spirit*. The deadness of so much subsequent psychology results from an inability to cope adequately with difference of level. From the rest of the *Philosophy of Spirit*, if you allow for some obsolescence, there is more to be learnt, I should say, than from any of Hegel's successors. I confess, on the other hand, that I am happier when I reflect on the larger scale structure of the dialectic, for one reason because there are long stretches of Hegel's speculation in which the obscurity deepens as the scale diminishes.

**AE.** What do you make of this notorious obscurity?

**E.** Sometimes I fancy that Hegel, like Aristotle, is thinking and writing with his whole system present and ready in his mind, and that wide implications of the particular point he is making constantly press in upon him, demanding expression. Being not a Greek always sparing of words in a lean athletic tongue, but a German writing in his diffuse and clumsy native idiom and caring nothing for his readers, he allows the implied context too much liberty to intrude. For that I blame him.

**AE.** I know what you mean. I sometimes think of him as a composer who hears all the overtones of the notes running in his head and tries to get them, too, down on paper, shattering staff notation in the process.

Yet one feels he knows his way through the dark forest. In the *Encyclopaedia*, when he was bound to have his pupils in mind, he is on the whole more intelligible, forthright, and more down to earth in the spiritual world, if one may put it that way.

All the same the dialectic is not always very convincing even above Nature. In the posthumously published lectures on aesthetics triplicity, assuming that it is not merely inserted by the note-takers, approaches a purely external notation, less plausible than Wittgenstein's decimals in the *Tractatus*. Yet you said that the triad signified not mere movement but eternal activity.

I did, but if form and content are one in dialectic, we must take seriously—perhaps more seriously than Hegel himself—what Hegel says of the unimportance of number above its own proper level,[1] and realize that dialectical triads can only symbolize the eternal in different degrees of remoteness.

I'm not sure I follow.

Look at it like this. It is absurd to remain tangled in the understanding and view the dialectic as a rigid formula, a procrustean bed of thesis, antithesis, and synthesis, to which all content must submit without resistance. What did Hegel really mean by identity of form and content? I've sometimes tried to think of the triadic series as like a musical theme in perpetual variation, or like the metrical base which is differentiated in immense diversity in poetic verse. The iambic pentameter, for example, has based a mass of English verse, rhymed and blank, but with what vast difference in the superstructure!

> Be wise today, 'tis madness to defer.

is poles apart in sound, rhythm, and sense from,

> Of Man's First Disobedience, and the Fruit,

but they are both iambic pentameters.

That's rather suggestive.

[1] See p. 57, above.

**E.** It's not altogether misleading, but it doesn't go very far. I see dialectic—and so it is meant to be seen—wherever I see lift from level to level; and to me lift from level to level only makes philosophical sense as the immanent activity of spirit, ultimately of absolute spirit. I agree with you that triplicity in the lectures on aesthetics, and sometimes elsewhere too, seems often no more than Hegel's way of imposing a convenient beginning, middle, and end on what he wants to say next. I find the historical system and the dialectical ordering of the arts suggestive; not necessarily final, but at any rate the series of art-forms from architecture to poetry is a scale on which difference of kind is very plausibly blended with difference of degree. I fancy I often spot dialectic quite vividly in a transitional passage of colour and shape in the context of a picture. The flash of it is nothing empirical—indeed no empiricist has yet said anything which touches the nature of art—and the fact that a picture is 'static' has nothing to do with the dialectic in it. In colour television it is painfully absent, because neither nature nor art has had a hand in putting the colours together. They never quite mate to breed glory.

**AE.** And how often do our horticulturalists violate the chastity of Nature. This age has no taste in colour.

**E.** And little sense of proportion. There is dialectic in great architecture; none in a modern tower-block. In music there is nothing else, though Hegel, hankering after thought in words, wasn't very sensitive to it; and music plays too little part in his conception of poetry, though seeing that German was his native tongue that isn't altogether surprising.

**AE.** You mean that spirit can make of colour and sound more than Hegel perceives?

**E.** Yes, it can give them much more ideality than he realizes. But to be fair to him we must try to estimate his inevitable limitations. Let's try to judge Hegel's philosophical industry as falling within his own Absolute, and let's furthermore take note of the position from which we attempt to criticize its truth. A philosopher is sometimes censured on the ground that his theory of knowledge precludes the possibility of his own philosophy. Kant is often thus attacked, and the question is a fair one. *Prima facie* it may seem a simple matter of deciding whether or no the thinker in the dock is guilty of self-contradiction, but if the case is at all complicated, I think it is fair that the critic should disclose his criterion, especially if, like us, he doesn't regard himself as observing *ab extra* from a realist's or phenomenalist's stable platform.

You want us to start by laying it down that both Hegel and ourselves, being only particles of absolute spirit, are subject to overlapping knowledge and ignorance?

Yes, but because we are particles, minor organs, of absolute spirit, there is in our knowledge an inkling of that in which we participate.

That is not question-begging?

Not if we can develop a vague inkling into some sort of coherent system. Remember that philosophy doesn't start with definitions. The inkling, as I have cautiously called it, has been very variously interpreted by different thinkers. Plato once tried to express it metaphorically as recollection. Descartes claimed that 'we' have innate in us the idea of a perfect Being. Hegel judged Spinoza, the *Gottbetrunkener Mensch*, an acosmist. Less philosophical theists have pinned their faith on everything from tribal gods to pantheism. Kant offers us non-constitutive Ideas of the unconditioned and a God true in practice but not in theory. Bradley posited a sentient Absolute above an intellectual middle-space.

What form does your inkling take?

First let me say that, like nearly everybody else, I live most of my life at half-cock, as I once heard the poet Kavanagh put it. Harold Joachim once said that one couldn't philosophize properly for more than about three quarters of an hour in the day. The 'weights of becoming' hamper us all. Still, I believe that now and again, when reason is awake in me, I glimpse something akin to Hegel's absolute spirit, but perhaps more often some rare human action or some splendour of art fills me with certainty that to regard this as merely finite would be absurd. Nature sometimes hints eternity to me but perhaps more often Nature in a landscape painting, or in the poetry of Keats, or in that of Wordsworth when Nature and not human beings is its subject. The face of Nature in all its shapes, beautiful, indispensably beautiful as they are, cannot compete with the art to which they give proximate matter. Or am I making a false distinction? Is any aesthetic appreciation of Nature a faint beginning of art?

**AE.** A slight concession to Croce?

**E.** Perhaps, but the point I want to stress is that our inklings of the Absolute in which we participate all differ because of the irregular overlapping of our knowledge and our ignorance. And yet, perhaps because of the overlap, our thinking remains self-critical.

**AE.** What do you conclude in respect to Hegel? Our knowing may contain an indeterminate inkling of the Absolute, but does that justify a claim to have displayed eternity in a system which rests on no presupposition?

**E.** I think it does. What else can a genuine philosopher attempt? Hegel in overlapping knowledge and ignorance glimpsed eternity as spirit single and timelessly active. He and his vision —this becomes more and more obvious as he works it out— were of course the product of the age in which he lived. He knew well enough that he could not escape from his own epoch, though he could enlarge it enormously. He grasped it, and lived it in thought as a back-reaching specious present far broader and deeper than any of his contemporaries succeeded in doing, indeed than any thinker in any age, had been able to do. With histories of philosophy, religion, art, and political world-history he recovered the past into the present, and not as merely factual but as spiritually significant. It was a colossal effort to see below the streaming transience of temporal process, and what could he do, I ask again, but follow the example of every true philosopher and try to express *sub specie aeternitatis* what he had seen revealed?

**AE.** Try to explicate it in a single dialectical whole?

**E.** Yes, but that was a task which on his own theory he could not perfectly perform, though he seems sometimes reluctant to admit it.

. Explain please.

. On his own theory, if I understand it, Hegel is a partial self-approximation in and as which absolute spirit constitutes itself. He has both reality and knowledge only in a degree. He can endeavour to set out his system as a dialectical circle innocent of presupposition and symbolizing eternity by its return upon itself. So much by way of form we may concede to his dim inkling of the eternal. But his only source of detailed content is the specious present of his own epoch. Rich though that is as he has grasped it, its finitude shows that the unity of form and content which he claims for the dialectical method can only be approximate.

. Could he not reply that as it descends through spirit and Nature, and individuality lapses towards self-externality, the dialectic *must* deteriorate, become looser, in form and content together?

. Yes; if thought and Being are not totally severed even at the nadir of spirit's self-alienation, then Hegel must mean just that when he calls Nature 'impotent'. All the same, he himself can only approximate to his own Absolute. Whatever place on the *Stufenleiter* he may assign to himself as the thinker in whom the philosophy of the past has so far culminated, he cannot anywhere, on his own hypothesis, apprehend complete truth. Even in the inkling of eternity which the immanent self-constituting Absolute gives him his knowledge and his ignorance must overlap. And here in passing let me again make a point which should be clear already. I am sure I follow Hegel in saying that in this inkling there is no implication of absolute spirit as a separate thing-in-itself. Its infinity rests on the absence of any such implication. Beyond its self-approximations it has no surplus reality. If *per impossibile* it had, its juxtaposition to its approximations would turn it finite at once, as has surely by now become obvious.

But if we accept Hegel so far as to admit that we, too, are only semi-real approximations, to what extent and on what grounds are we in a position to criticize his system? We can say that many of his dialectical transitions in spirit, and even more in

Nature, seem to be based not on opposition but on mere difference, and consequently do not convince us that they exclude possible alternatives. But that was to be expected if the dialectic was bound to get looser as it descends to the relatively self-external, though one might wish that Hegel had been more frank about it. Besides that, we could show that the speedy advance of science, which is, I suspect, a function of its object-world's self-externality, would demand a considerable reconstruction of the already rough dialectic of Nature. As to history, I think it was only sometimes that Hegel's enthusiasm for a Germanic protestant world almost made him believe that freedom was now finally achieved. I fancy he did not think that civilization was likely thenceforward to change a great deal, but he remarks more than once that of the future there is no knowledge, only hope and fear. We today, I suppose, are less sure that there has been quite such a progress of freedom as Hegel believed. I can think of no one who would have been more amazed and horrified than Hegel by either Nazi Germany or communist Russia. In general he overestimated the permanence of his world, because he thought it good.

**E.** It is not the permanent, not what he took to be long-lasting, that matters in Hegel. It is the immanence of the eternal which he managed to grasp in so much of the transient; it is the dynamism of the dialectic which keeps one alert to the rise or fall from level to level in all experience. Nor do I greatly care how much the dialectic, in order to remain one in form and content, may deviate from a formal pattern which expresses well enough the main-scale unity, opposition, and reconciliation of thought and Being. Hegel perhaps tries to cling too firmly to that pattern. Though he was hostile to the pretentions of formal logic, I fancy he retained unconsciously a touch of its formalism.

**AE.** Doesn't that often happen? I think the British idealists, especially Bradley, retained more of the empiricism they were combating than they supposed.

**E.** That is probably so.

**AE.** We have now admitted, I take it, that whatever blameworthy mistakes Hegel may have made, his dialectical system could not have been perfected by himself, nor could be perfected by anybody else in a subsequent age. The understanding can from hypothetical premisses achieve a limited precision, but precision beyond what the understanding contributes in its sublation by dialectical reason could not be achieved by the speculation of one epoch.

. If absolute spirit constitutes itself of imperfect approximations to itself, that must be so.

. Then what we owe to Hegel's dialectic will be a vision of spirit's omnipresence which is not precise with the precision of the understanding, but is rational and not merely based on myth, and beyond that such stretches of the dialectic as after a century and a half still seem to us sounder than subsequent speculation.

. I agree in principle, but let me amplify. As regards the omnipresence of spirit, I would like to revive an old controversy between the Oxford idealists and their empiricist opponents on the subject of terms and relations. Looking back, I fancy that neither side fully understood the other's assumptions. Roughly speaking, the empiricists held that relations are external, that they do not enter into the terms they relate. Indeed, if the terms related are atoms or self-enclosed monads, as on the whole the empiricists have held, they must be mutually independent, unaffected by the relations between them. If aggregated, they will still remain untouched, in no way determined by the heaping, which seems to be the only sort of togetherness permitted. Moreover these impenetrable singulars are taken as independent not only of the relations between them, but also of the singular experient who apprehends them, whether he takes them as real or phenomenal. Independence of relations and independence of thought go necessarily together. There is no 'original' unity of thought and Being in the terms and relations of the empiricists. For Bradley, on the other hand, relational thinking belongs to his intellectual middle-space above immediate feeling and below a sentient Absolute. This thinking is self-contradictory, for relations are both internal and external. If you take them as completely internal, the terms lose all difference from one another and the relations vanish; if as completely external they lose all relevance to their terms. To me the significant point, which I think Bradley might have made clearer in the posthumously published fragment on relations, but which his opponents would mostly not have understood if he had, is this. A relation can only be internal to its terms within a whole which unites thought and Being. Outside thought, in an object, I mean, which is alleged to be independent of thought, there could be no passage of mutual determining between its terms. Significant negation, difference within identity, which is what the internality of relations rests on, has no place in a world aggregated of atoms or monads. Such a world, if it could exist at all, would be meaninglessly positive. Hegel has to my mind shown that thinking spirit is immanent wherever there is identity in difference, and that is everywhere.

**AE.** The contradiction between internal and external at the relational level might have suggested to Bradley a dialectical ascent into a rational rather than a super-sentient Absolute into which thought passes by a suicidal leap.

**E.** But it didn't. I thank Hegel for giving me a better grasp of the difference between understanding and reason. Meanwhile there are one or two topics we promised ourselves to come back to. I'm thinking in particular of the final triad of spirit: art, religion, and philosophy.

**AE.** And we've rather tended to shirk error and evil. But I think we've talked enough for today. Let's adjourn till tomorrow.

**E.** Very well.

# VIII

## THE FINAL TRIAD. ERROR, EVIL, TRAGEDY, AND HISTORY

We noted yesterday that Hegel sees the dialectical movement through his final triad as smooth development rather than as passage through sharp contradictive opposition. We saw with some slight puzzlement that all three final phases of spirit have the same rational content. This content is, in fact, Absolute Idea, the supreme category of thought, in which cognition and volition are one. Art is its presence in sensuous shape as the Ideal; in religion it is embodied in pictorial thinking blended with devout feeling; in philosophy its true nature is manifest as rational thought.

And, as you suggested, development of form without development of content seems hardly Hegelian.

I did suggest that, though I then made some defence of Hegel against your charge of jugglery.[1] All the same he does seem inclined at this level to develop form without developing content. I get too giddy at these heights to dogmatize, but I would have expected Hegel to say (and hoped he would say) that the easy dialectical transition has meant that aesthetic and religious experience are cancelled but also preserved to contribute their own peculiar intrinsic values to the *Wahrheit* of philosophy, thus definitively distinguishing reason from understanding. But he appears, unlike Schelling, to regard art as a relatively transient moment of the human spirit. Perfect, in the sense of perfectly genuine, art belonged, he believes, only to the ancient Greeks, because in their sculpture (the palmary instance) the sensuous and the spiritual (here the Olympian gods) are balanced in perfect interpenetration. He sees the *Weltanschauung* of the Greeks, before Socrates made them think, as predominantly aesthetic.

[1] See pp. 118–9, above.

**AE.** He clearly didn't know much about either ancient Egyptian or oriental art.

**E.** He didn't. In Christian romantic art, for all its greatness, which Hegel, despite his passionate Hellenism, fully acknowledges, the sensuous and its spiritual embodiment can no longer be in balance. Christian art is ancillary to religion, and the growing secularization of art in his own day suggests to Hegel that art is dying, and that what is wanted is rather an advance in aesthetic theory than more works of art. After that dreary conclusion, which seems to me a covert lapse from reason towards understanding, one is bound to wonder whether religion is genuinely preserved as well as cancelled in Hegel's philosophy, or whether as art appears to be simply superseded by religion, so religion, if Hegel could have dared to say so openly, is due for sheer supersession by philosophy.

**AE.** I rather doubt that. Hegel always sounds quite sincere when he talks about religion, even when he isn't abusing the Roman Church. I have a different idea. I suggest that when he decides that only Greek art is perfect art he comes near to recognizing that the incidence of artistic genius in history is not a single steady development in progressive stages. No doubt art varies to some extent concomitantly with the development of the human spirit in other fields, and Hegel believed that philosophy, religion, and political freedom had, at any rate in the west, all by a single line of progress reached a joint climax in his own epoch. But that was blatantly untrue of art. He couldn't have thought—indeed he suggests the contrary—that the art of his own day was an improvement on the best of the past. Rather he would have agreed when Hazlitt wrote (he may even have read it): 'These giant sons of genius . . . tower above their fellows, and the long line of their successors does not interpose anything to obstruct their view, or lessen their brightness.'[1] 'Very well, then!', Hegel might have said to himself, 'let us preserve the general notion of spiritual progress by switching art, which has always at its best and in its essential nature had a religious content, completely and without trace into religion.' I would, like you, more happily differentiate reason from understanding if I

---

[1] 'Why the Arts are not Progressive', *Morning Chronicle*, 1814.

thought I had Hegel's sanction in believing that both art and religion were preserved in it. But although you said that Hegel ought to allow human philosophizing its specific emotion,[1] I nevertheless remember that feeling, though markedly and *essentially* present in both aesthetic and religious experience, is for Hegel only an empty subjective form which is almost bound to vanish in his conception of philosophical thought. So perhaps Hegel's philosopher, like Plato's God, must be denied the weakness of emotion.

. When the owl of Minerva flies at dusk, and the philosopher paints in grey on grey the shape of a world grown old, does he paint with feeling? Frankly I don't know, but I am only trying to expound Hegel in order to find out what I can accept from him. That is massive, but it certainly does not include the death of art. His interweaving of the history of art with its specific forms is full of good things, though his dialectical ordering often seems arbitrary and sometimes to be sinking towards mere classification. He is trying to give objective content to the empty subjectivity of Kant's reflections on aesthetics, just as he had tried to amplify and complete Kant in the field of ethics, and he gives us generous measure in both spheres. His enthusiastic Hellenism affords him, in my judgement, a sound basis here as in all his thinking. You may not always like his taste in painting, and his comprehension of music was very poor, but he was an intelligent and sensitive critic of poetry. The fault I find here ties up with his urge to swallow art and possibly religion in thought. Though the Ideal in art is beauty, his criterion in each art-form is too intellectual. I am rationalist enough to believe that you must exalt no form of experience above thought, but as regards other forms, if you cannot sublate them wholly in pure reason (and you cannot), you must allow a degree of autonomy to their less perfect form of rationality. You mustn't treat them as poor relations: your philosophy will suffer greatly if you do. But I wander.

. Well, let's hear more of what you think of Hegel's general conception of art.

. I am sure, as I have said, that art is rational and yet autonomous,

[1] See p. 119, above.

that it is not transient and that its content need not be religious. There is no substitute for it. I think Hegel well expresses the status of a work of art as an object. It is not a merely material existent but a pure appearance midway between the immediately sensuous and ideal thought. 'The sensuous in the work of art', says Hegel in the Lectures on Aesthetics, 'is itself something ideal, but which, not being ideal as thought is ideal, is still at the same time there externally as a thing.'[1] I would agree, too, that in the interest of ideality the thing must be visible or audible.

**AE.** Come, come. What about Berenson's tactile values? And what about the taste of a great wine? Doesn't that at least border on the aesthetic? Yes, and don't forget the remark of Souvestre in *Le Philosophe sous les toits:* 'Le café tient, pour ainsi dire, le milieu entre la nourriture corporelle et la nourriture spirituelle.'

**E.** Perhaps. There were gods in Heraclitus's kitchen.

**AE.** And there were angels dining at the Ritz, but no matter.

**E.** Anyhow I agree that this lifting of the sensuous to the level of spirit is ubiquitous, and I give you your coffee and your wine. It is analogous to the dialectic of body and mind, which we discussed. I said just now that I could sometimes sense dialectic in a passage of colour and shape in a picture. In poetry the full significance dawns and develops first in the sound and then in the sense of the words, though that dialectic is perhaps in the end circular. If you don't realize that you will never discover why you suddenly find some poetry so astonishingly perfect. The notion that thoughts in prose or images in poetry have arrived stark naked and have had then to be clothed with words is utter nonsense. Searching for the right word is trying to complete a thought. Language is an activity, not a store of second-hand garments collected in a dictionary. But again I wander.

**AE.** I like Hegel's analysis of the sensuous in art better than Croce's view of a work of art as an intuition-expression prior to the distinction of fancy and fact, because that compels Croce to exclude the material thing from art altogether and make it a purely

[1] Hegel, Jubilee Edition, Vol. 12, p. 67; Knox, Translation, p. 38.

economic means of communication. But now tell me, what have you gained from Hegel's treatment of religion?

. I'm not sure. In great works of art in any form from architecture to poetry—even on occasion in ballet—I can sense absolute spirit without any qualm of doubt, even with something like worship: if you called me a Bardolater I shouldn't resent it. I can sense it, too, in the life and sayings of Jesus of Nazareth, but I am not sure that with me that is a religious experience. I feel the reality of religion less in sermons or ritual than in poems, and then much less in the epics of Dante and Milton, though both were far greater poets, than in some lyrics of Donne and Herbert. I do, at the same time, find it of great interest that to Hegel, unless I have misunderstood him, Christ is much more real in the consciousness of Luther and the Reformers than he was in the minds of the somewhat superstitious apostles. That seems to bear out my own suggestions about life beyond the grave. Hegel was certainly a modernist, and it is not surprising that Croce should have said of him that he was at once the most religious and the most irreligious of philosophers. On the other hand, I learned something from Hegel's lectures on art and religion which my classical education under Christian teachers had not taught me. I discovered that there was a fair degree of reality in the deities of the ancient world, even, despite disreputable episodes in Homer and Hesiod, in the Gods of Olympus. I have admitted that I have no great religious susceptibility, but I perceive that the Gods, one or many, are not purely fictitious, and that to believe them to be so is to misapprehend spirit. There is no escape for thought from Being.

. So the heathen weren't just bowing down to wood and stone. Hegel clearly attracts you as a rationalist thinker and aesthetician rather than as a protestant Christian. I might attack you again on that subject later. Meanwhile let us dwell for a little on the darker side of life. We have not as yet said much of error, evil, and suffering.

. I haven't much to say about error. It is parasitic in the sense that it must have truth to pervert, though truth is the conquest and supersession of it. Hegel holds that the more profound a man's genius the deeper his error if he errs, and the greater his wickedness if he sins.[1] Doubtless he is right.

**AE.** 'Corruptio optimi pessima.' That recalls not only Plato, but also Luther's 'Esto peccator et pecca fortiter, sed fortius fide et gaude in Christo.'

**E.** Clearly, and the Luther quotation links up closely with Hegel's conception of sin; but I would like to talk about suffering first. In Hegel's view pain pervades all human life. It is the privilege (*Vorrecht*) of all that feels, and the higher the feeling nature the more intense can be its unhappiness and pain. Nothing great is achieved without pain and passion. Pain is the tension of desire, which expands and becomes sharper as the level of the sufferer rises. It may begin with ordinary hunger and thirst, but it can rise to the 'unhappy consciousness' in which the worshipper finds himself at once infinite and finite, one with God, yet struggling in an agony of severance. In the pain of desire—and all pain is desire—the subject is barred by a limit in himself from a wholeness which ought (*soll*) to be his.[2] This is the moment of obstructed feeling in the ideality of the finite as it strives towards self-realization, the moment of limitation and exclusion in a man's individuality. Writ large, it is the contradiction in absolute spirit's self-alienation, and it is symbolized for Hegel in the passion of Christ.

**AE.** That strikes me as profoundly true. It is, I suppose, what has been called Hegel's pantragism?

**E.** Yes, but the connection of tragedy with pain and evil in the sense of wickedness is an extension of this doctrine of Hegel's, which I'd like to try to explain, because I incline to accept it.

**AE.** I have an idea the trouble starts in the Garden of Eden.

**E.** I think so.

**AE.** Adam and Eve, tempted by the serpent, ate of the fruit of the tree of the knowledge of good and evil. This was sin, and as punishment they were exiled from the Garden and had to

---

[1] Cf. Hegel, Jubilee Ed., Vol. 16, p. 184.
[2] Ibid., Lexicon, s.v. *Schmerz*.

exchange their idle innocence for a life of toil in conflict with the serpent.

. But was it really sin? In Hegel's very acute interpretation of the tale,[1] if they had never eaten the apple they would never have grown up from a state of immediate naïve innocence and started to labour towards their destiny of genuine reconciliation through double negation; which means, if you substitute the symbolized for the symbol, the Protestant faith.

. Hegel seems a bit ambiguous here. He thinks the legend wrong in attributing the sin to the contingent intervention of the serpent: rather sin is 'original' in man, and was bound to break out. So we have to assume that the eating of the apple *was* a sin, the sort of sin, I suppose, that Luther recommended. In any case, without this outbreak human life would, as you say, have been singularly futile and lacking in interest: happiness has no history. I doubt if Milton grasped this point.

. He quite obviously didn't. There is a clash here, not between right and wrong but between two rights. Hegel is quite sure what ordinary straightforward wickedness is. It is to will and intend the finite, to be wholly subjective, pursuing one's own selfish aims to the uttermost, seeking only one's narrow singular self. I think we might say that the wicked man *aims* at individuality by exclusion, and that this necessarily entails perversion. But that sort of wickedness is merely tedious, and straight wickedness was not the guilt incurred by Adam and Eve. Their apple-eating was deemed a sin, and a punishable sin, but the sin and its punishment were both indispensable for the future of mankind. You quoted Luther aptly, and Hegel must have known the saying.

. Adam's punishment seems fairly consistent, too, with Hegel's doctrine that legal punishment rehabilitates the criminal as a subject of rights, after he has violated right in himself and universally, not merely in his victim. It was really Adam's life outside Eden that made a man of him. But how does tragedy come in?

[2] See *Encyclopaedia*, §24, *Zusatz ad. fin.*

**E.** Hegel thought poetry the supreme form of art, and tragic drama
the supreme form of poetry. There I think he was right as
against Croce's universal lyricism. I don't believe Shakespeare
would have achieved his amplitude as a poet, his insight into
every corner of human nature and his unparalleled power of
individualizing it, if he hadn't been a man of the theatre. Hegel
was fascinated by the concept of moral responsibility as it
appears in Greek tragedy. It differed clearly enough from the
ethics of his own day, but it greatly influenced his view of
world-history.

**AE.** You mean, for example, that Clytemnestra had a duty to kill
Agamemnon for sacrificing Iphigenia, but Orestes also had a
duty to kill his mother, and he had a bad time from the Furies,
although Apollo and Athene eventually got him pardoned and
purged by the Areopagus?

**E.** Yes; there lies the source of tragic conflict. If you killed a close
kinsman, even with strong justification, you were polluted with
a guilt which you had to pay for, quite likely with your life. The
plainest case is Sophocles' *Antigone*, so much beloved of Hegel.
Antigone obeys the nether gods, the gods of the family, by bury-
ing her brother slain in battle against the state. Creon, her uncle,
by forbidding the burial, obeys the laws of the state, and
thereby the Gods of Olympus. Because they are each loyal to a
one-sided duty, the wholeness of justice is broken in two. It
reasserts its unity by the death of Antigone on the one side, and
of Creon's wife and son on the other. This is the essence of tragic
drama. There is surely more than a touch of it in the story of
Adam and Eve, though Hegel doesn't expressly say so. He does,
however, find tragedy a significant factor in world-history.
Innocence-sin-punishment appears as an inescapable triplicity
—only a stone is innocent, we are told—but the sin remains
ambivalent. Only a year after the presentation of Sophocles'
*Oedipus Coloneus* occurred the trial and execution of Socrates,
and there Hegel thinks that the guilt lay on both sides. There
was a clash of two genuine loyalties. Socrates was teaching the
young men to think and to criticize the old gods. It was the
first crepuscular flight of Minerva's owl, and the citizens of
Athens had a right, or a half-right, to defend the old happy
Greek immediate unity of religion, art, and patriotism.

. Perhaps they had, but since you mention the *Oedipus Coloneus* and the *Antigone*, let me remind you that the gentle Sophocles does not weight the scales evenly. He has deep pity for the blinded Oedipus, and Creon is the only man in Thebes who doesn't believe Antigone to be wholly in the right. She becomes of heroic stature in the modern sense of heroic. Even the old men with their traditional choric caution shake their heads at her only for resisting Creon's authority, not for any sin against the Olympians. And Sophocles has to make Creon a quite hubristic tyrant in order to justify his appalling final peripety.

. I agree, but there is still a genuine tragic conflict in both those plays. They would not otherwise be so profoundly moving. Even Bernard Shaw, unlikeliest of tragedians and a hater of Christian cruelties, managed to impart real tragedy into *Saint Joan*. In one form or another these things happen, and Hegel rightly signalizes the element of tragedy in the rise and fall of successive nations which marks the progress of freedom in world-history, and in the destiny of world-historical men who do not know that a cunning 'Providence' is shaping their ambitions and actions to its own ends.

. However one may criticize in detail the adventures of Hegel's *Weltgeist*, this dialectical pantragism gives him a much better basis for historical valuation than the partisan historian can show, or the eunuch chronicler who supposes that a recital of bare facts can excuse him from passing judgement.

. Emphatically. I would even say that Hegel's recognition of the clash between old and new, the tragic conflict with right on both sides between the half-consciously motivated action of the world-historical man and the current morality of his age, contributes more and shows a more profound insight than his dialectical build-up of the state in the *Rechtsphilosophie*. For his state he had, after all, a pretty good foundation in Plato's *Republic* and Aristotle's *Ethics* and *Politics*. He had, perhaps a shade regretfully, to meet the expansion from a Greek *polis* to a modern nation-state by introducing subjective freedom with 'civil society', but he kept the state as organic as he could.

. Yes, Hegel is always the disciple of Plato and Aristotle, for

whom the state exists by Nature as the real prius of the individual. You can see why the *Weltgeist*'s progressive phases are
nation-states when Hegel criticizes the remoteness of government
in the dead immensity of imperial Rome, and when he attacks
the loose congeries of heterogeneous communities which constituted the German Empire of his own day.

**E.** Especially when he condemns the feudalism which persisted in
the German Empire, because it meant the forced dependence of
the weak on the strong, and the lack of any adequate legal basis
to protect the vassal from his overlord's oppression. The state is
reason, the feudal condition is caprice. I find Hegel's state sound
enough compared with theories of the state which regard it as
little more than a convenient mechanism for protecting the sort
of liberty which J. S. Mill believed in, but I am more interested
in the human individual than in the precise nature of the state.
I find more impressive the light which Hegel's *Philosophy of
History* throws on the development of ethical principle beyond
the private morality and *Sittlichkeit* of the world-historical man's
contemporaries. Despite the superficial criticism of even such
competent liberal historians as H. A. L. Fisher, there is nothing
here brutal or cynical. There is, however, a tough, unsenti-
mental attitude which may or may not have helped to inspire
German megalomania in the next century; but that would have
shocked Hegel quite as much as it shocked the critics who
blamed him for it. One doesn't blame Wagner because Hitler
got drunk on *The Ring* and probably thought himself very like
Siegfried.

**AE.** No. The cardinal instance in which the *Weltgeist* crushed the
old right under the new was, I suppose, the crossing of the
Rubicon. Caesar defeats Pompey and overthrows the corrupt
Roman Republic.

**E.** Cato's suicide was tragic, but much more so was the murder of
Caesar. Caesar was ambitious and Brutus was an honourable
man, but most of us would say with Hegel that Caesar's was the
higher right, and that the prolonging of his rule could have
been a great benefit to Rome while Octavius waited in the
wings.

**AE.** Don't start spinning hypothetical history. It gets one nowhere.

Too many alternatives become possible as soon as one begins. History is about what *did* happen.

I. In general I agree, but one's vision of history cannot altogether exclude contingency, and it is not irrelevant, especially when one reflects on certain crises, to speculate on what might have happened. Don't give me eunuch history.

I. Oh well, I suppose Wellington's comment on Waterloo was an historical statement. But come down to brass tacks and answer me this. Hegel believes that you can infer from the history of the world that its progress has been the necessary rational course of the *Weltgeist*, the gradual progress, that is, of human freedom. He also says that in tracing world-history, *Wir haben historisch, empirisch, zu verfahren.*[1] In other words his attitude here pretty well parallels his attitude to natural science in the *Philosophy of Nature*, and I would have thought that reason ought in history to find less contingency opposing its insight than confronts it in the 'impotence' of Nature. Well then, does Hegel succeed or fail?

I. I would have thought that the contingency of human caprice would make history harder to rationalize than Nature, where reason is rudimentary but not perverted. In natural science, moreover, unless you are concerned with evolution, you haven't got to dig up a past which is always questionable in terms of mere fact. But before I try to answer your question, we've got to realize the limits of the field within which it makes sense to ask it. Hegel begins by cutting out from the sphere of world-history America, Africa bar Egypt, and portions of Asia. China and India are broadly characterized, but he finds them too spiritually static to manifest the *Weltgeist*. History really begins for Hegel with ancient Persia and its religion of light, and closes with Europe tolerably peaceful after the disappearance of Napoleon from the scene and the firm establishment of Protestantism in its northern regions. Slavery and serfdom were clearly on the wane. Universal freedom really did seem to be dawning. Given his religious beliefs—or the religious factor in the philosophy in which he certainly thought he had contained and crowned all previous philosophy—Hegel was almost bound

---

[1] Jubilee Ed., Vol. 11, p. 36. Sibree, Trans., p. 11.

to see his own age, especially in the florescence of spirit in Germany, as the climax of a rational process in time. Yet just before the end of his lectures on Universal History he remarked cautiously, 'Bis hierher ist das Bewusstsein gekommen': 'Thus far has consciousness reached'. He had no belief in prophecy, and he thus confesses that he has produced only, as Collingwood called it, an interim report. Yet an interim report implies that there is more to come. Once Hegel commits himself to revealing the march of spirit in time, he and we cannot wholly overcome the spurious infinite in our vision of history. We are bound to see what we know of it as an interlude between an indefinitely back-reaching past and an unending future. Reason in this temporal field cannot fully sublate pictorial thinking, or the element of contingency which already appears in Hegel's selection of only some nations as hitherto world-historical. But like most of us, Hegel thought it absurd to seek no sort of rational pattern in history. You couldn't expect him to look on the birth of a world-historical hero as a mere biological accident, or to accept Balzac's 'Les miracles du hasard auquel on doit les grands hommes.'

**AE.** No, I couldn't; but although I'm anxious to hear your answer, I would be glad to postpone it in order first to consider just why the Balzacian view is wrong. It implies, I suppose, an indefinitely extended pedigree behind the great man, full of marriages and begettings, any one of which for a thousand reasons might not have happened. It implies at a lower level of abstraction a highly erratic continuity of the germ-plasm, since the zygote which grew into Julius Caesar was a union to which there were countless possible alternatives right up to the instant of conception. Yet Hegel asks us to view the emergence of Caesar as more or less freely necessitated within the march of reason in time.

**E.** I've got no new answer beyond the general principle we have been so far following, but perhaps it's worth rubbing in again. Your three levels are all levels of temporal process, even Hegel's dialectic of history. They are all stages or phases of approximation to absolute spirit, terms in a developing series such that the truth, the *Wahrheit*, of each is to be sought in the level above, and the fault or defect of any level has its source in levels below.

. We saw that exemplified when we discussed levels in the individual man.[1]

. We did, but let's now begin with your lowest level, the purely ontogenetic account of Caesar's birth, and consider it by itself in abstraction from the *Stufenleiter* to which it belongs. Caesar as an aggregate of cells then appears as a chance result, contingent on the one side, and on the other a product of blind *a tergo* necessitation. It is, moreover, the result of a spuriously infinite process which has no determinate beginning. It signifies nothing except in application to presupposed entities. It is a condition, but nothing approaching a sufficient condition, of their existence. Its only connection with Julius Caesar is that it somehow subserves his Being; precisely how we cannot say, because in our apprehension of contingency there is necessarily a factor of ignorance. We do, however, at least know that an assault from below on a man's cellular constitution—the daggers of Brutus and Cassius, for example—is the way to kill him. If we go up to what I might call your pedigree level, we still don't reach a coherent system within which we can account rationally for Julius Caesar. For blind necessitation and contingency we now substitute the vagaries of human caprice and all the changes and chances of human life. Men and women are more individual than cells, and there is an element of will in their behaviour, but they can't predetermine how they will fall in love, nor, save to a small and mainly negative extent, what sort of children they are going to produce. They know even less of the lower, subserving, level than does the biologist. Moreover, the serial process of mating and begetting is virtually a spurious infinite: it goes back through all the generations of mankind and all the stages of man's evolution. Human life so viewed does not make the sense that human reason demands. By logical necessity, I suggest, Hegel sets the eternal to work in the temporal. But that, as I said, does not enable him to exclude all contingency and ignorance.

. Thank you. That makes it clearer, and I return gratefully to my question. Has Hegel, subject to those qualifications, shown that from ancient Persia to his Germanic world of 1820 or thereabouts, human freedom has widened and progressed, rationally

[1] See p. 101 above.

manifesting absolute spirit? Is that the verdict of *Weltgeschichte* as *Weltgericht*?

**E.** I wouldn't doubt that Marathon, Thermopylae, and Salamis were victories for organized freedom over loosely integrated tyranny. I would not doubt that the Greeks knew that some were free, whereas Xerxes only knew that one was free. Nor of course would I quarrel with Hegel's (not wholly original) view that Greece, or at any rate Athens, reached a far higher peak of civilization than Rome and exerted a much more lasting spiritual influence than Rome, though largely through Rome. But the glory of Greece biased Hegel's judgement. He grossly underrates Roman poetry. He regards law and the recognition of the legal person as almost Rome's only contribution to civilization, and he thinks it was the deadening effect of the imperial government's immense distance from the life of the private citizen which prepared a ready way for Christianity. Was that really the march of reason? I wonder, despite your healthy fear of hypothetical history, whether the western world might not have had a happier and not less rational history if Julius Caesar had lived to conquer and discipline those tiresome German tribes as effectively as he conquered the Gauls and set them on the road to civilization. At least the Germans might have developed a more comely, latinized language.

**AE.** We shouldn't have had Hegel.

**E.** We might have had somebody even better.

**AE.** You don't think the German tongue was the indispensable medium of Hegel's thought?

**E.** I do not, though I used once to try to believe it. I now applaud a remark of Bradley that every German thinker should be compelled on pain of death to write in French, in order that when he began a sentence he should have to know how he was going to end it. I admit, too, that I am a shade sceptical about that *gemütlich*, deeply inward, loyal and meditative, but slow and rather unpractical native of the German forests. Still, that's more or less how he seems to have appeared early in the nineteenth century to his foreign contemporaries such as Mme. de Staël and Balzac, so perhaps he did once exist.

. What about Hegel's rather robust attitude to war?

. He does suggest that the discovery of gunpowder has human-
ized war because you no longer have to see at close quarters the
man you are shooting at. Could he have envisaged any other
instrument of change? Had he any choice on the evidence but
to regard war as a probably ineliminable factor in human
nature and as certainly inevitable in history up to date? War
for Hegel is only a part of what in the Preface to the *Phänomenologie* he calls 'the seriousness and suffering, the patience and
toil, of the negative.' In any temporal manifestation of absolute
spirit in which the will is involved (not least in religion) the
first negation in dialectical movement is essentially destructive
and painful.

. And I suppose blind? You're thinking of a phase of revolution
like the Terror, in which nobody can envisage a *positive* issue?

. Yes, but the 'suffering and toil' is not simply erased in the
'second negation', if it comes, as Hegel thought that on the
whole it must. He sees freedom, in its true and proper sense of
self-determination and possession of one's own real nature, as
only to be achieved and enjoyed through a real struggle (even
a struggle *through* slavery) in which men have faced death
deliberately and are ready to face it again in order to retain
their freedom. Freedom not so won seemed to him a thing of
little value.

. No better than the calm and idle innocence of Eden. Men must
have been much battered and exhausted by life to have invented
that legend.

. For Hegel the conquest of the negative is the essence of *all*
spirit, finite or infinite. In the 1820s this reasonably courageous
view of life and death would still have been generally accepted.
The decline of slavery and serfdom was perhaps sufficiently
widespread in world-historical countries to make plausible
Hegel's belief that ultimately right is might, and that so far
civilization had progressed rationally towards freedom. As to
war, I would invert a famous saying and put it thus: 'Woe to
that man by whom the offence cometh, but it must needs be
that offences come.' I have seen more war, and at considerably

closer quarters, than Hegel. In two wholly unjustified aggressive wars launched by Hegel's compatriots Germany was
defeated. That was a triumph of reason over barbarism so
abysmal that it seemed to shatter any notion of reason's dialectical progress. There had been little moral ambiguity in Bis-
marck in 1870, much less in the Kaiser in 1914, and in 1939
none whatsoever in Hitler. Twice, millions of lives were destroyed in the agonizing effort to restore the *status quo ante*. In
both cases victory was simply the cancelling of a very horrible
negative and no more. No consummation, no synthetic result,
could emerge. Yet even in those wickedest as yet of all wars a
trace persisted of war's virtues. Total war can hardly be recommended as a tonic for stagnation, yet despite the cost of it in
blood and pain we were wholesomely braced for a season. There
was patriotism wholly unchauvinistic, friendship and complete
mutual reliance intensified in the strong supporting bond of
discipline, and the comforting discovery by so many ordinary
men that fear is controllable and courage a cultivable habit.
There were flowers, too, of a high and selfless courage which
rarely blooms except in war. There was nothing brutal in the
two or three V.C.s I have known. I don't forget that those who
suffer in war are the crippled and the bereaved, but I confess
that when I heard a certain noble and reverend pacifist say on
TV—or was it in Hyde Park?—that he wouldn't mind if the
armed forces of this country were abolished, what flashed across
my mind was the story of Origen.

**AE.** Origen?

**E.** He was a third-century Christian apologist and a very distinguished theologian. He was anxious to be ordained a priest, but
in order to escape the sin of fornication and to continue safely
the teaching of the female sex, he had castrated himself. The
Church refused him ordination. He was made a presbyter, but
the appointment was subsequently cancelled.

**AE.** I should indeed hate to see society gelded of its sailors, soldiers,
and airmen. They're getting few enough anyway. I once saw a
weary procession of pacifist marchers resting in Hyde Park. I
wished I could surreptitiously surcharge their 'Ban the Bomb'
banners with '*si vis pacem para bellum*', as a gesture in favour

not of war but of peace through the balance of threat and counter-threat as at least better than no peace at all; and before we leave the subject let me support you by saying that to compare the courage of a conscientious objector to that of a man who voluntarily leaves a loved wife and family to fight for his country—Oh yes I've heard it claimed that he is just as brave— is absurd and not a little disgusting. But you really think, do you, that two world-wars have refuted the notion of reason in history? On the side of unreason, indeed, you have got to throw in more than half a century of horror in Russia, which has surely been a more savage and longer-lasting denial of freedom than ever occurred before. Since the enslavement of the Balkan states it has been a horror self-enclosed and barricaded against reason, but it shows every sign that it may soon explode and spread its self-generated poison, like all tyrannies, in the name of liberation. Potentially it is worse than Nazi Germany. If Solzhenitsin records fairly, Soviet Russia falls scarcely short of tyranny as Godwin and Shelley pictured it.

*Monstrum horrendum informe ingens cui lumen ademptum*; in this case the light of reason and humanity. Hegel *redivivus* could only swallow Hitler, Stalin, and Stalin's pretty faithful successors by saying once again that the *Weltgeist* is not in a hurry. That may be the not very comforting answer. Croce, I seem to remember, says that good and evil are too closely bound up together to permit either optimism or pessimism in the long term, but does that hold when ideology, after sixty years in full control of education and the media, has perverted reason in hundreds of millions of minds, so that the doer of evil believes that what he does is good? As Solzhenitsin acutely points out,[1] Iago knew he was wicked and only moved by hatred, but the ideologically possessed fanatic does not. The Inquisitors and the Jacobins passed away under external pressure, and German repentance, after defeat, has seemingly been in the main sincere, but could Russia repent short of losing a nuclear war which would probably leave no world for anybody to repent in? I confess I sympathized when, during the last war, the head of the War Office M.I. country section concerned with Russia said to me he wished the Soviet and German armies would totally destroy

---

[1] *Gulag Archipelago*, I, English trans., pp. 173 ff.

one another. I wonder whether future historians will find much difference between the *détentistes* and the *munichois*.

**AE.** And what about China? Certainly I see little joy and little reason in either a nuclear war or a flabby collapse before communism. I don't think I can find a better way than Hegel's of looking at the past from *his* point in time. Moreover, the notion of reason he leaves us with is pretty well the criterion by which we condemn Hitler and Stalin. Since Hegel I can see no obvious pattern. Set beside his hierarchical conception of things, the general egalitarian trend of mankind seems merely to caricature the progress of freedom. In Russia it speedily provoked an opposite tyranny. It may do so elsewhere. Do we see a new and larger-scale dialectic taking over? Is there reason in it? It looks very grim and primitive, suggesting ancient theories of history as cyclical repetition rather than Hegelian dialectic.

**E.** Maybe. Meanwhile its time to end this rather inconclusive talk. Tomorrow to fresh woods——

**AE.** No, to the old *selva oscura* of Hegel's Logic, however *selvaggia ed aspre e forte* we may find it.

# IX

## LOGIC AND PANLOGISM

I'm not perfectly sure I have a satisfactory answer to the charge against Hegel of panlogism, nor even that I can make clear to myself just how Hegel conceived the relation between the Logic and the rest of his system.

So you will take refuge behind the inevitability of human ignorance?

I may in the end, but I shall fight to the last, because I believe that Hegel's Logic, though I'm not quite certain what it is, was his greatest achievement. The important fact about it, the thing which makes it unique, is its ontological character. It is a logic of objective thought, whereas the two theories of thought which the word 'logic' would have most naturally signified to Hegel were both logics of subjective thinking, namely the formal logic which has descended from Aristotle's *Prior Analytics* and survived with little change for two millenia, and the transcendental logic of Immanuel Kant.

Why d'you think formal logic has survived so long?

Perhaps because it is so teachable. Schiller the pragmatist once said to me, 'Philosophical logic', by which he meant chiefly Bradley and Bosanquet, 'is unexaminable nonsense, formal logic is examinable nonsense.'

To Hegel, I suppose, subjective thinking would mean the thinking of the understanding, thinking at a level where the object is taken as independent of thought by the finite thinker, who judges and syllogizes more or less in accordance with the rules of formal logic, but must rely for material truth on experience, *Erfahrung*?

Yes, formal logic can guarantee validity if you obey its rules, but no more.

**AE.** And Hegel saw Kant's categories, too, as principles of subjective thinking?

**E.** Yes, though, rude as he was about them, they certainly pointed the way for him. You might say that as compared with formal syllogism, which demands of reality no more than that it should be capable of being quantified and classified, the Kantian categories are semi-ontological. They do not characterize real Being but only its appearance, only phenomena. They do not derive from experience, but they are empty till experience gives them a sensuous filling. They are *a priori* only inasmuch as they impart its structure to the understanding of each singular individual thinking subject. Thus they are merely principles of subjective thought. On the other hand, they do impose on a phenomenal world this same categorial structure, which renders that world more or less coherent, despite the presence in it of no more than mechanical *a tergo* necessitation, and the consequent indefinite regresses and antinomies which proclaim its phenomenality. So we might perhaps even allow that thinking in Kant's phenomenal world is quasi-objective, if we could overlook his failure to tell us how the phenomenal objects which each one of us establishes come to constitute a shared phenomenal world. No doubt there was an escape route from solipsism for Kant through his transcendental unity of apperception, but he didn't take it. It was left to Hegel to discover and exploit the universality of the 'I'.[1]

**AE.** Yet Kant obviously provided him with his main stepping-stone to a logic of objective thought. I suppose he owed more in general to Aristotle than to any other predecessor, but in this field he borrowed little from Aristotle and the formal logic which descended from him.

**E.** He regarded formal logic as an elementary but reputable enterprise in the natural history of thought. Figures of syllogism, he thought, were at least better worth discovering than new varieties of veronica. He points out that Aristotle never used syllogism to express his really philosophical thought, and he does in his own Logic accord subjective thought its subordinate place as a moment sublated in objective thought: he dialecticizes the

---

[1] See p. 25, above.

forms of judgement and syllogism to constitute 'Subjective Notion', the first main-scale phase of his logic of the Notion. The logics of Bradley and Bosanquet draw largely on Hegel's 'Subjective Notion'. Hegel was of course familiar with Aristotle's view of the 'laws of thought' as primarily laws of Being, and with the Aristotelian categories, but he does not seem to be aware that in the *Posterior Analytics* Aristotle works out a theory of scientific syllogism which reflects what he believes to be the real structure of Nature. It is a logic of truth, that is to say, not a formal logic of mere validity and class-inclusion.

. How does it work?

. Aristotle believed the sublunary world to consist of an immutable system of genera and species in which certain necessary properties inhere. Each genus is, ideally, the province of one special science, and the *infimae species* of which the genus consists are the starting-points of scientific demonstration, but they are themselves not demonstrable but directly intuited.

. I'm not sure I follow.

. Well the *infimae species* are the genus actualized, developed to concreteness, through a series of determining differentiae down to the final differentia, below which there are only logically indiscriminable singulars. The hackneyed example of an *infima species* is the genus animal gradually differentiated until it is fully actualized by the final differentia, rational, which gives you the *infima species* man. The *infima species* is viewed by the mature Aristotle (not the young Aristotle of the *Categories*) as logically indivisible and better entitled to be called substance than the singular individuals, which it defines, giving their essential nature as opposed to the accidents which spring from their matter. But the *infima species*, the concrete actualization of the genus, is indivisible and is indemonstrable: it must be intuited by νοῦς.

. This is the isolation of intuition from discursus which we criticized in our first talk?

. It is, but I dwell on it here because Aristotle holds that νοῦς in its immediate grasp of its incomposite and therefore indivisible objects (which in fact include also elements above the sublunary sphere) is one with them. Obscure and fragmentary as is what remains to us of Aristotle's doctrine of νοῦς, this is the first real spark of objective idealism.

**AE.** Where does demonstration come in?

**E.** The first and basic step in scientific demonstration is proof that a certain property inheres necessarily in an *infima species*, and the proof is a syllogism in Barbara: the property as major term is shown to inhere in the species through the middle term, which is the differentia, the cause of the inherence. Aristotle provides no example. A hackneyed medieval illustration to fill the lacuna is, 'Man *qua* rational is capable of laughter.' The proven property then serves as middle term in an episyllogism to prove the necessary inherence of a second property, and so on. The ideally complete special science would reveal all the *infimae species* of the genus, and from each would depend a linked series of necessary properties. The logical structure would thus reflect the structure of Nature, for the series would be 'close-packed', as Aristotle puts it, meaning that each property would be *immediately* linked to its predecessor, i.e. to the proximate cause of its inherence. I should add that not only certain axioms but also the purely nominal definitions of the properties are also intuited, but the true definition of a property is the demonstration of its inherence turned round: laughter is a property of man *qua* rational.

**AE.** Then Popper's muddle, to which you referred,[1] was between definition of the substantial *infima species* and definition of a necessary property, which is a demonstration turned round?

**E.** Exactly. Now the point I have been over-long in making is this. Every nexus of terms in a special science thus ideally demonstrated would be universal and necessary. Science admits no singular term, and for Aristotle the distinctive characteristic of the universal, τὸ καθόλου, is necessity, not generality, which is a mere corollary of necessity: if a species X is necessarily Y, all its specimens are Y, but allness is not what science is concerned with.

**AE.** How does the formal logic of the *Prior Analytics* connect with scientific demonstration?

---

[1] See p. 96, above.

. That was an attempt to elicit some sort of order and system out of everyday argumentation, and it doubtless also sprang from a desire to equip Lyceum students for public speaking and disputation: rhetoric had been an early interest of Aristotle. But the *Prior Analytics* opens with the announcement that the subject to be investigated is scientific demonstration. We only get to that in the *Posterior Analytics*, but the scientific syllogism in Barbara, which we've been discussing, is the norm to which all the weaker figures of the *Prior Analytics* approximate in different degrees. Barbara, Celarent, Darii etc. is a dirge in medieval notation, the elegy of form degenerating to the mere class-inclusion without which formal validity even in symbolic logic is not possible. No singular term appears in these weaker syllogisms—that Socrates *qua* man is mortal is not an Aristotelian syllogism—but terms are construed in extension.

. You talk of degeneration, but perhaps Aristotle thought it would be good for his students to approach scientific demonstration through a course in formal logic; how dreary it must have been. Anyhow Hegel might have given Aristotle more credit for an attempted logic of truth than he did. Having established this Aristotelian and Kantian background, can we now attack Hegel himself?

. By the time Hegel began to construct the *Science of Logic*, he had the foundations of his system firmly in mind. He was a monist and a rationalist. He conceived the universe as absolute spirit, and he conceived absolute spirit as an eternally active unity of thought and Being. This activity one can only express in temporal terms as a *prima facie* contradiction: it is at once self-developing and self-developed, self-manifesting and self-manifested. Within this unity thought at its highest meant to Hegel thinking (the thinking of absolute spirit as subject) in which will is sublated, cognition which has 'provoked' volition as its negative and determining opposite, and now contains it in dialectical return upon itself.

. So that the analogue in theological imagery of absolute spirit would be God in whose omniscience omnipotence is absorbed?

. I would think so, and it may be helpful to remember that Hegel, wearing his theological spectacles, calls logic the exposition of

God in his eternal essence prior to the Creation,[1] and sees the Creation as no arbitrary parergon of God but as his total and unreserved self-determining, his self-creation without which he would not be God.[2] Hegel's problem as a logician was to express the universe in terms of pure thought, but as a metaphysician to do it without so stressing the identity of thought and Being as to obliterate the difference in favour of thought. In other words he must avoid panlogism, though I doubt if the danger of it occurred to him.

**AE.** The whole question, then, turns on what specific kind of identity-in-difference the unity of thought and Being manifests.

**E.** Well, does it? It is the identity-in-difference of the universe—that is why Hegel calls it 'original'—it is not a specific type actualizing a generic nature. Thought is not a genus, nor, as Aristotle observed, is Being. The original unity of thought and Being is unique; it is neither specific nor even *sui generis*. The relation of genus and species does not here apply.

**AE.** If the unity of thought and Being is unique and, like the objects of Aristotle's νοῦς, incomposite and indivisible, how is the question of panlogism ever to be decided? The only way I can think of would be to set the categories of the Logic beside the contents of the rest of the system, and try to see the difference as it would seem to have appeared to Hegel.

**E.** We shall have to do that, but I would like first to make a point about the identity of thought and Being which sometimes escapes notice. The dispute between idealists and realists has too often been narrowed to the question whether or not the objects of the mind's thinking and knowing exist in independence and unaffected by being thus objectified; i.e. whether or not Being is independent of thought. To the question so put there is no straight answer, because you cannot separate the two terms so as to verify the dependence or independence of Being. But that is only half the question. One must ask at the same time whether thought can *be* in independence of Being: the relation between them, whatever it is, must be reciprocal. And surely

---

[1] *Science of Logic*, Jubilee Ed. Vol. 4, p. 46.
[2] Cf. *Philosophy of Religion*, Jubilee Ed. Vol. 16, p. 53.

the answer is clear: it is only in judging and interpreting the nature of Being that the thinking mind constructs itself and *is*. To urge that Being in total severance from thought is not verifiable is perhaps not a decisive argument against a correspondence theory of truth, but a mind which can think without an object, like a mill turning without grist, is surely a quite unintelligible non-entity.

. You say that only in its active commerce with Being the thinking mind *is*, and that the idea of a mind which can think without an object is nonsense. If thinking mind *is*, and if the relation between thought and Being is reciprocal, you can surely now claim that Being is thought, and claim it without risking a charge of panlogism, because if thought swallowed Being without trace, thought could not *be*. In fact you can now say, I think, that thought and Being are each the whole unity, and that is clearly Hegel's doctrine.

. A rather fine-spun argument, but I think sound. My trouble is that to me, now, though it was not always so, the identity of thought and Being seems so simple, basic, and 'original', that I find it hard to excogitate arguments to prove it. To call Being the *alter ego* of thought is the best way to express the 'original' unity.

. It must be if spirit is essentially self-conscious. Can we now turn from the identity to the difference?

. Let's hear Hegel himself. In *Encyclopaedia*, §24, *Zusatz* 2, which seems pretty reliable, he says, 'In logic we have to do with pure thought, the pure thought-determinations.' This means, I imagine, that thought in the logical categories is pure (*a*) in contrast to all other forms of awareness. In *Zusatz* 1 he had said, 'As thought constitutes the substance of external things, so it is the universal substance of what is spiritual. In all human [sc. sensuous] intuition there is thought. So, too, thought is the universal in all imagings (*Vorstellungen*) and acts of recollection; in short in every activity of the spirit, in willing, wishing, and so forth.' Thus thought in the categories is in its own true and proper form, not depressed to the lower approximative forms in which its nature is veiled. But it is also pure (*b*) *qua* abstract. In the *Science of Logic* he says, 'Philosophical thinking in general is still concerned with concrete objects, God, Nature, spirit; but logic is concerned with these thoughts *as thoughts* in their complete abstraction.'[1] In the same work he says, 'The realm of logic is truth unveiled (*ohne Hülle*) and in and for itself (*an und für sich*).'[2] But in the *Philosophy of Spirit* he says that thought in logic is *wie es erst an sich ist*, as it is initially and implicitly.[3]

**AE.** I would think that in your last quotation Hegel is looking forward to Nature and Concrete Spirit, whereas in the penultimate one he is looking down from the pure thought of the Logic to the lower, approximative forms of apprehension. Incidentally, if we call the lower forms approximative, I suppose we must say that pure logical thought constitutes them in its immanence, and that they, reciprocally, go to constitute pure thought?

**E.** That must be so within the whole ambitus of absolute spirit's self-diremption and self-reconciliation, but I would point out that the lower forms of awareness emerge from the yet lower levels of Nature, and the series of them rises through objective spirit, art, and religion to philosophy, which then starts to express itself as logic, because it cannot properly be thought of as the summit and goal of the series save as the completed circle of Logic, Nature, and Concrete Spirit. Hegel's circular architectonic cannot precisely articulate eternity for all his mighty struggle to make it do so. Hence a good deal of his obscurity.

**AE.** No doubt, but can't I still ask what is the difference within the identity of Being and the pure thought of the Logic?

**E.** In trying to answer you I may stumble, and you must regard nothing I say as dogmatic. The transition from the Logic to Nature, where with Space and Time begins an ascent up to Philosophy, is a transition from the 'what' of the universe abstractly expressed in pure thought, to its 'that', which Hegel conceives as thought's necessary self-externalization. It is a transition within *Wahrheit* from the subjective moment of truth in the narrow sense to its objective moment of reality or genuineness,[4] and the 'that' is not a mere point of attachment

---

[1] Preface to second edition, Jubilee Edition, Vol. 4, p. 24. I follow Miller's translation of a slightly obscure passage.
[2] Ibid., pp. 45–6.   [3] *Encyclopaedia*, §467.   [4] Cf. pp. 21, 35–6, 45–6 above.

nor a purely self-identical and unvarying substratum: it is an all-pervasive developing moment. To suppose we could gain access to sheer Being by bursting through, or by somehow circumventing, a screen of thought is absurd, because in supposing this access and contact we are already presupposing thought. Being is not a 'that' without a 'what', but a moment 'over-reached and grasped', as Hegel puts it, within all thinking. In science and everyday thinking we do in a sense extrude it, because in those fields we reflect—indeed we go to constitute—absolute spirit in its self-alienation. Though our object-world is ultimately our other self, we apprehend it there only as other and not as self. Yet that world in all the detail of it which we know by acquaintance, in all of it which we infer as context, and in the final fruit of our mind's universality, our inkling, that is, of its transcendence beyond our finite ignorance—all that world is a structure, or more truly a constructive activity, of thought.

:. I am convinced, but it is difficult; largely, I think, because it is very hard to grasp the 'original' identity of thought and Being as unique in nature. One tries vainly to equate it with specific types of identity in difference. Hence so much incomprehension of Hegel. But I am beginning to realize that other types of identity in difference necessarily presuppose it.

:. Perhaps you also find it hard because of the immediacy in which human experience starts. We as men trying to grasp the fulness of *Wahrheit* cannot escape, first, an immediacy of feeling in which subjective and objective are not yet differentiated, and, next, the severance of them which reflects the self-alienation of absolute spirit. We can only apprehend this transition and ascent—the fusion of 'what' and 'that' and its development—as a process in which, to begin with, thought is sunk in the sensuous; a process, moreover, which presupposes natural levels lower than sense. A subject's distinction of itself from a 'real' object only emerges as thought begins to mediate sensuous feeling and break up its dim promise of self-consciousness, and thenceforward for a season, as we saw, the subject assumes its object to be detached and independent. Man at that level builds up a world which starkly confronts him. He can to some extent alter it by practical action, though he can nowhere create or annihilate absolutely, but it is still a largely miscellaneous and self-external world. His subjective thinking, his understanding of it, is hypothetical, all borrowed premisses and loose ends. It owes such unity as it possesses to the dawning of universality in and as his mind, but it is still a very dispersed and unconcentrated construction. He will insist, if challenged, on the half-truth that it is not mere thought but real Being. But he remains unaware that such form and content as he finds in his object is *eo ipso* the form and content of his own mind in so far as it has reached universality. Science achieves a measure of unity in its departments, but no over-all unity, because its attitude of detachment is still that of common sense. All the principles and laws of the understanding, all the articulations and characterizations of reality which science apprehends, it grasps and must grasp as objectively real, although equally all of it without residue is scientific *thought*. When Hegel from a philosophical and not a scientific point of view orders the main structural elements of science dialectically as the categories of Essence, they are pure and abstract, but they quite obviously refer to an externally real world. When he shifts the metaphor from God's mind and symbolizes the Logic as the realm of shadows, I am tempted to think that he means the shadows cast before them, so to say, by the more concrete though less pure realities to come, viz. Nature and Concrete or Manifested Spirit.

**AE.** I am now fairly well convinced that Hegel neither intended panlogism nor fell into it unawares. We may dismiss the charge, because the prosecutor entirely fails to grasp the 'original', the primordial, identity in difference. He assumes that thought, essentially and as such, is subjective, that the transition to Nature is simply fraudulent, and that Hegel is hypostatizing subjective, essentially subjective, thought and claiming it to be the universe. But I'm still a bit worried about sense. I don't need to be told again that there is no sense-perception without interpretative thought, but if you withdraw thought from sense-perception, distilling the essence of it into categories, laws and lesser universals, is there no blind, alogical residue? I am sure you can't perceive colours and sounds without at least rudimentary judgement, but there is surely a non-intellectual element there, too?

Yes, but not a ready-made sense-datum waiting for you. When thought is just beginning to emerge, our experience is ambivalent, and language reflects this: many thinkers use the words 'intuition' (notoriously Kant) and 'perception' without being very sure whether they mean by them act (or passion) or content, and they are apt to slide out of one meaning into the other. Below that stage, or at least when you get below feeling, there are merely natural phases from which a man only knows he has developed after he has grown up and reflected. But of course these natural phases contribute. The continuity is not broken. Developed through and as corporeal feeling and sensation, and then lit by thought (I can't improve on the metaphor) they contribute all the rich stuff of our sensible world and of our emotions, and they are preserved in sublation to the summits of human experience. That I am sure, is Hegelian doctrine, and Bradley's anonymous but obvious slap at Hegel about the sensuous curtain being a cheat which conceals no more than an unearthly ballet of bloodless categories[1] was entirely uncalled for. These natural phases, on the other hand, belong to the development of Being *within thought*. Remove them from the overreaching grasp of thought and they vanish in darkness. Your blind, alogical residue belongs to the natural, or perhaps we should say the subliminal. As long as we avoid the sense-data myth and the error of supposing sensation to be a form of knowledge, I don't think it much matters where exactly we place your residue. If we let a faint dawning of thought into it, we might find there Hegel's categories of Quality.

When you say that the natural phases belong to the development of Being *within thought*, you mean, I take it, as viewed by the philosopher, not as falling within the thought of the adult man or the scientist?

Yes; to the latter the natural phases would fall within a detached object-world.

All right, I accept your disposal of my alogical residue. On your showing, a man is really the product of development down three lines. He grows (*a*) from the zygote, and is (*b*) thereby linked to

---

[1] See *Principles of Logic*, 2nd edn., p. 591.

a line of ancestors which evolution traces to something ape-like; but (*c*) he comes to be and develops by virtue of spirit immanent both in him and in Nature from which he rises. And it is only (*c*) which makes (*a*) and (*b*) possible.

**E.**  Man has in fact a material, an efficient, and a final cause. One conclusion to be drawn is that the truth, the *Wahrheit*, of man, as of all else that is true, lies always ahead. That is why I am so sure that a man's individuality depends far more on inclusion than on exclusion and limitation, and why I don't believe in singular immortal souls.

**AE.**  One might here draw a social anti-snob moral, too: it matters much more where a man gets to than where he comes from. I seem to remember Bradley wondering in a fierce footnote somewhere why some people objected to being descended from an ape if they didn't mind growing from a sperm and an ovum. But can we now before we end take a quick look at Hegel's categories with an eye on what they foreshadow?

**E.**  Very well. To begin with, remember always that there is no naked Being to which the categories might be supposed to correspond. You can get at Being through various forms of thought, but you will nowhere surprise it in a state of thought-less nudity. What Hegel's categories foreshadow is concrete thought, the degree of real Being overreached and grasped by reason pure and reason sublating the lesser forms of awareness, namely understanding and, if I follow Hegel, the *Intelligenz* which is present in sensuous experience and hardly yet to be called *Verstand*. If there is any relation here which we might call correspondence, it is between the categories, the abstract *Denkbestimmungen* of the Logic, and the *Begriffsbestimmungen*, as Hegel calls the conceptual determinations which overreach and grasp Being in Nature and Concrete or Manifested Spirit. Secondly, bear in mind that the categories are abstract thought, but thought makes all things what they are, constituting itself in constituting Being as its other self. Logic must therefore be a single structure commensurate with the universe; and if the universe is self-othering, that structure must be a single dialectical system. Any dialectical system, moreover, since it is self-developing, must be, as Hegel vehemently insists, form and content in one. The categories are abstract, but they are not empty forms sterile until they receive a kiss of life and creativity from an intake of sensuous manifold *ab extra*.

In Hegel's eyes, then, Kant erred triply. His mere dozen of categories are not linked in system; they yield no knowledge even of phenomenal objects till fertilized by the unknowable; yet they permit finite singular minds to think subjectively without an object and to no purpose as if, to borrow your simile, they were mills turning without grist.

Nevertheless, apart from The Greeks, Hegel owed more to Kant than to any other thinker, even Spinoza.

I'm sure he did. But to return to our muttons. I still don't feel quite happy about this abstractness of Hegel's categories. The original unity of thought and Being, as I now reflect on it, seems to me at once obvious and enigmatic. You said that Hegel's circular architectonic couldn't precisely articulate eternity, and I begin to wonder whether the difficulty of relating Hegel's Logic to the externally existent world, the difficulty which led to the charge of panlogism, may not arise from an inevitable imprecision in Hegel's exposition. If thought and Being are each the whole unity, how far does that go towards justifying Hegel in abstracting thought for separate consideration?

He certainly could not have set out his system in any other way. He was bound to expound thought as a developing series, and the circular return upon itself of the series was, I think, as near as any man could get in presenting the eternal. Even apart from its detailed finitude as the product of a particular epoch, Hegel's system, being human thought, could not do much more than *suggest* absolute spirit's moment of total timeless self-concentration. I have called the dialectical triad the *minimum rationale*, because its moments must be thought together. In Being—Not-being—Becoming, you can perhaps nearly achieve this, but you can't think the whole system, the super-triad, completely together, and your failure is not just psychological.

You mean that the circle is better than the straight line, but it is still linear. What you say helps me to make my point. I agree that Hegel had to try to display thought in abstraction in order to explain what he meant—to himself, I fancy, as well as to his readers. But was not this abstraction of thought from Being only a pedagogic necessity? Was it not a dissection which doesn't murder but does distort, though it perhaps distorts less than any other philosophical system?

**E.**  You may be right. I told you to take nothing I said as dogmatic.

**AE.**  I promise not to. Can we now look into the correspondence between the categories and the *Begriffsbestimmungen*?

**E.**  *Infandum, regina, jubes renovare dolorem.* By that I only mean that often before I have sweated blood trying to sort out this problem. I'll try to give you an idea. It'll take a little time although I shall abbreviate and omit. I might even lapse into nonsense. In Hegel's Logic abstract thought culminates in Absolute Idea, which is the identity embracing the abstract thoughts subjective-and-objective, theoretic-and-practical, true-and-good. This consummation the Idea reaches thus: 'It posits itself as the absolute unity of the *Begriff* and its reality (*Realität*), and thereby collects (*zusammennimmt*) itself into the immediacy of Being. Thus it is the *totality* in this form——Nature.'[1]

**AE.**  A little explanation, please.

**E.**  The *Begriff*, which is commonly translated 'Notion', covers the third and final section of Hegel's categories. The form of each of these categories is the complete triad, the *minimum rationale*, the thought which returns upon itself. The first of them we have already discussed. It is the concrete universal, the universal specifying itself to concrete individuality. The Notion develops through Subjective and Objective Notion, and all its phases (I dare not get entangled in their detail) are phases of self-conscious thought. The *Realität* of the Notion, and the immediacy of Being into which the Idea collects itself, must surely refer to Being as external reality; but it is slightly confusing to find that in the previous paragraph Hegel has said, 'Logic in the Absolute Idea has returned to the simple unity which its beginning is', and then goes on to explain that Absolute Idea, or the fully self-comprehending Notion (they are the same thing), is now in simple self-relation, and so through mediation,

---

[1] *Science of Logic*, last two pages.

or rather through the sublation of mediation, returns to the first category, Pure Being, as to an equality (*Gleichheit*) to itself.[1]

Meaning that the Logic has come full circle. All that, though, is movement in the medium of pure abstract thought. It reminds one of Aristotle's God thinking his own thinking.

I don't doubt Hegel had that in mind. He had fully assimilated Aristotle's *Metaphysics*. In fact he ends the *Philosophy of Spirit* with a long quotation from Met. Λ.

But if we are still within the circle of abstract thought, how does Nature get in? It apparently did not get into the self-conscious thinking of the Aristotelian God.

Absolute Idea is clearly another name for the thought of perfection—so far has Descartes's 'idea in us of a perfect Being' travelled—and I fancy Hegel holds that with Absolute Idea closing the logical circle the transition to the externality of Being in Nature is *eo ipso* accomplished. We have reached a total perfection of subjectivity, metaphorically the mind of God before the Creation, which must determine itself in a total objectivity. The transition, says Hegel,[2] is not a product of becoming or an ordinary dialectical transition. The Idea freely releases itself, and 'by reason of this freedom the form of its determinateness is also utterly free—the externality of space and time existing absolutely for itself without subjectivity.'[3] That is how Nature exists, he continues, in externality for mere consciousness, but in the Idea it remains in and for itself as the totality of the Notion and, in relation to the divine knowing of Nature, as science. The last remark means, I take it, that Nature can be philosophically dialecticized.

That's very interesting, and it's not so obscure as many commentators seem to think. I don't believe you've talked nonsense. There may be a touch of pedagogic necessity, but I think the transition follows from the unique original unity of thought and Being. In perfected thought the overreaching and grasping of Being must be contained.

It is very much a reconstruction of the ontological proof of

[1] Ibid.  [2] Ibid.  [3] Ibid.

God's existence, which Hegel defends against Kant's unimpressive hundred-dollars argument.

**AE.** Yes it is. What can we now say about the correspondence of categories and *Begriffsbestimmungen*, which get their name, I suppose, because every phase of Nature, philosophically viewed, must have some touch of the Notion?

**E.** That's right, but I'm not sure 'correspondence' was the right word. Anyhow we must first sketch in briefly the categorial series between Pure Being and Notion. The Idea goes forth freely into Nature, but if the transition is self-liberation it is also self-alienation, and the return of spirit through Nature must begin at the bottom. The Logic is the triadic form writ large. The categories of Being are thought in an immediacy which gets its first negation in the categories of Essence, and in the categories of Notion thought, explicitly self-conscious, returns to itself as result containing its process. Being (the thought of Being, that is) divides dialectically into Quality, which we discussed,[1] Quantity, and Measure (or Proportion). In Measure Quality and Quantity, hitherto mutually indifferent, unite in mutual determination. In all these categories of Being thought is naïve and unquestioning, surface without depth. The *prima facies* is all the truth there is. One would expect thought here to be the *Intelligenz* inherent primarily in sense-perception, but Hegel locates in Quantity and Measure the categories involved in mathematics, which has its own kind of *a priori* and uses sense-perception only as a spring-board, and he calls mathematics a science of the understanding. But the ambiguity doesn't much matter.

**AE.** And what of Essence, where Hegel, I suppose, has mainly in mind everyday thinking and the special physical sciences?

**E.** There thought loses its innocence. It begins to mediate, to distinguish between sensuous appearances and the universal essences which underly them, and it finds this distinction, which it is the function of the understanding to elicit and establish, grow steadily more contradictive. Hegel in Essence reconstructs dialectically many Kantian categories, and whereas Kant's

---

[1] See p. 80, above.

categories are more or less disconnected single thought-forms, empty till the alogical sensuous fills them, the categories of Essence are not, indeed, each a triad like the categories of the Notion, but each a duality of thought reflecting the first two moments of the triad in mutual contradiction. This contradiction sharpens as the moment of appearance develops from mere show (*Schein*) to the accidents of Substance, the effect of Cause, and finally to equipollence with its essence in Action and Reaction, or Reciprocity. At that point thought is passing to self-determining freedom from the mechanical *a tergo* necessitation and indefinite regress which beset all the categories of Essence, even Cause and Effect, because they are the categories of the understanding's finite world. We are on the threshold of the Notion where the concrete universal replaces, sublates rather, the abstract universals which are offered by the understanding as essences but are never genuinely commensurate with their particulars. The doctrine of Essence is hard, as Hegel himself admits. Besides Kantian categories and other principles of scientific thought, it contains principles of other philosophies which, in Hegel's view, fail to rise above understanding to reason. The dialectic is often obscure and sometimes, I would think, arbitrary; yet if you look at a table of the categories of Essence you will easily recognize the progress of development between, for example, Thinghood and Substance. Moreover, it was part of an heroic and novel attempt to bring together and systematize not the figures and modes of validity but the ways in which men really do think objectively, however dim their awareness of the principles inherent in their thinking. Hegel was, too, the first thinker to perceive that this could not be done without making logic metaphysical. Yes, the Logic is a masterpiece, a masterpiece of genius. But we must get down to Nature. Before we talk about correspondence, we had better consider what a poor sitter for a philosophical portrait Nature is in Hegel's eyes. She is contemptibly innocent, and she enshrines no inner mystery to be reverently sought for. Her degree of *Wahrheit* is low, very low even as compared with sinning humanity. And in case the doctrine of degrees of reality may still seem to you paradoxical, let me here insist for the last time that it is a paradox only if you believe that Being abides naked and thoughtless.

**AE.** No, it no longer strikes me as paradoxical; but I don't blame you for insisting, because it does flout common sense, as indeed philosophy usually must.

**E.** Good. The fact that Nature is only semi-real shows in its self-externality, its impotent juxtaposition of contingency and mechanical necessitation which fails to synthesize them in true freedom even in the natural life which is Nature's peak. Such is Nature as a semi-real object-world, and the thought which in the first instance overreaches and grasps its Being is consequently no more than sense-perception and the understanding which *does* detach Nature from itself as naked and thoughtless. At its best on its own level, this subjective thought is embodied in the natural sciences, which strive to penetrate the perceptual surface and systematize Nature in classes, principles, laws of her behaviour, and so forth. But sense and understanding do not have the last word on Nature. As she confronts the understanding, Nature is the non-spiritual, but she is, as Schelling put it, spirit frozen or petrified. Hegel uses another simile to express what we might call Nature *qua* pre-spiritual. 'The aim of Nature', he says, 'is to commit suicide, to break through its husk (*Rinde*) of the immediate sensuous, to burn itself phoenix-like, in order to issue from this externality rejuvenated as spirit.'[1] So Idea, which freely released itself to spatio-temporal Nature, must develop from this utter self-externality, in and through Nature, to explicit spirit. But, as I said, the thought which in the first instance overreaches and grasps Nature is only understanding subserved by sense-perception, and reaching its best in natural science. Now it is Hegel's view that the philosopher of Nature must respect science, which alone can supply him with his data, and that he must not in his dialecticizing distort the findings of science. This gives one to think. If Nature is the Idea in utter self-alienation and otherness, its impotent dispersedness and self-externality belong to it by logical, or ontological, necessity. That means that no science, whether it be the science of Hegel's time, or the science of our own or any subsequent epoch, can apprehend Nature (which in the present context we may extend to cover the cosmos) as a fully coherent whole. That scientists might accept, but it also

[1] *Philosophy of Nature*, *Zusatz* to final section.

means that philosophy of Nature, receiving its material from science, can only be rough and approximate. The dialectic cannot develop with the free necessity with which Hegel supposes his Logic to develop from Pure Being onwards.

**E.** But you don't believe that Hegel's categories develop through every stage of the Logic with incontestable certainty, do you?

**E.** Indeed I don't. But I do think the development of thought in its own abstract medium is nearer to truth than it could possibly be in any philosophy of Nature.

**E.** That would imply that there is no very close correspondence between the categories of the Logic and the *Begriffsbestimmungen* of Nature.

**E.** That is the conclusion I was coming to. The first triad of Nature is Space, Time, and Matter-and-Motion. You might call this the first effort of Nature to pull herself together out of utter self-externality, and you might say it echoes Being—not-being —Becoming and the subsequent early categories of Being in their naïve fluidity. Again, there is a frequent echo of the categories of Quantity in the pre-organic phases of dialecticized Nature. But these echoes of the Logic come, as it were, brokenly through the medium of less pure thought-forms. There is no one-one correspondence. Hegel manages to elicit a rough dialectic of the gradual self-concentration and individualization in natural forms. We pass from his first section, which he labels Mechanics, to Physics, and finally to Organics. In an earlier version the first section is labelled Mathematics and covers Space and Time, which Hegel, like Kant, tends to connect respectively with geometry and arithmetic, and Mechanics is pushed up into Physics. In this ascent the reflection of the Notion grows less dim, and there is some echo from the Logic of Objective Notion, which divides into Mechanism, Chemism, and Teleology, and is followed by Life as the first category of Idea. But I do not know how to correlate these categories at all precisely with their analogues in Nature. I rest convinced with Hegel that 'spirit gives itself a presupposition in Nature',[1] but my conception of Nature is largely pictorial thinking not raised

---

[1] *Encyclopaedia*, Part I, §239, *Zusatz*.

to a scientific level, and I prefer to enjoy her rather than spend a great deal of time investigating her philosophical origin and status.

**AE.** On the whole you have my sympathy, but you've talked so much that latterly I've hardly been allowed to get in a word. Tomorrow, when you tell me we talk for the last time, I shall stand up for my rights before I disappear.

**E.** Do your worst.

# X

## LAST WORDS

**E.** I shall celebrate our last encounter by attacking you from two incompatible points of view. To begin with, did you do well to abandon Christianity?

**E.** I didn't exactly abandon it. Even if Christianity is waning it has so permeated and moulded the civilization in which I partake that I couldn't possibly divorce myself wholly from it, unless I became a fanatical atheist, which at my age is unlikely. I simply became unable to accept as literal fact the Church's transformation into myth of the very marvellous, but not miraculous, life and death of Jesus of Nazareth. I have never been able to see anything spiritual in the notion of a miracle; that is not how spirit expresses its immanence. The Christian faith, which has been, I suppose, the most important factor in the history of western civilization, has done much conspicuous evil; but it has probably on balance done much more good, more humbly and less obtrusively, by spreading its gospel of love. Myth has its effective degree of *Wahrheit*, and if love at its best is not rational I have gravely misconceived reason. The world would be—probably will be—a great deal worse off without Christianity. I assure you I get no pleasure at all from seeing it dwindle and fade for all the wrong reasons, and I am dumb if you ask me whether I have anything better to put in its place for the mass of mankind. I doubt if it can be rationalized without losing half its motivation. I accept the need of religion, even as myth, if only as a basis of morality. I revere the humanity of Jesus and the nobility and tenderness of Christian teaching at its best; and also the virtues of many saintly Christians. It is merely that I am not very susceptible to the inspiration of spirit in that form.

**E.** An intelligent priest, wanting to convert you, would probably not argue but challenge you to go and live as nearly a Christian life for a year or two as you could, and then see if it didn't change your mind.

**E.** Religion is largely practical, and I'm sure that if I could take your priest's advice it would make me a much better man, but it wouldn't make me believe in the Resurrection.

**AE.** Very well. Christian theology is outmoded myth so far as you are concerned. Isn't Hegelianism almost equally out of date? Is absolute spirit any better founded than the Trinity? Hegel's philosophy is very much a sublation of Christianity, and they should surely pass away together, abdicating in favour of empiricism's more modest and safer attitude to truth and reality. Or take up linguistics. Be with it.

**E.** The sublation is to my mind what matters. If I were made that way, I should probably have been at least as good an Anglican as Hegel was Lutheran. To infer that, because myth is not historical fact, the universe is therefore not spirit, is a quite barbarous *non sequitur*. One philosophizes to try to lighten 'the burthen of the mystery', an end to which empiricism and linguistics do not greatly contribute, to say nothing of symbolic logic. I said long ago that I claimed only a degree of truth for my convictions. Had I ever been persuaded that they were quite false, I should not have espoused the modesty and security of these *ersatz* substitutes for philosophy. I should have deduced the plain nullity of philosophical speculation, which was perhaps the real conclusion not only of Hume but, had he confessed it, also of Wittgenstein. I should then have tried to make a living in some other profession. I said what I thought of the empiricists twenty years ago in a book called *Retreat from Truth*. I don't think they or I have since changed significantly. They are still to my mind barking up the wrong trees. As to your frivolous *tout passe, tout casse, tout lasse* attitude to Christianity and Hegel, I entirely repudiate it. I am less sure of progress than Hegel, as I have already indicated. I still believe that truth has survival value, but I begin to doubt whether between old and new on the one hand, and on the other good and bad, any universal and necessary connection can be detected. It is a doubt which art critics as well as philosophers should entertain.

**AE.** The *avant garde* takes the one view and the collector of antiques the other. Anyhow, so much for my polemics. You are stubborn. Is Hegel the only thinker, after Joachim, who has seriously helped to 'constitute' you, if that's the way you like it put? You wrote a book about Aristotle, and our talks have indicated that you owe him quite a bit. I would have thought that Plato had influenced you a good deal, too.

. Both Plato and Aristotle helped more than any other thinkers to 'constitute' Hegel—he regarded them as 'the teachers of the human race', perhaps more particularly Aristotle, who was the great systematic thinker of the ancient world as was Hegel of the modern. Without Aristotle and behind him Plato, there could have been no Hegel. So they both came to me through Hegel. But of course I had already absorbed a great deal from both of them directly. Aristotle survives, alas, only in the form of very concentrated lecture-notes—notes, that is, for his own lectures, not notes taken by listeners—and now and again one may be reading a précis of doctrine put together, like Hegel's *Encyclopaedia*, for his colleagues and pupils to read. Cicero speaks of the golden style of his dialogues, but of these only small scraps remain. This made me feel that I was learning at a great distance from my teacher's personality, but I got my first profound impression of a logically articulated universe and of an enormously powerful and comprehensive mind steadily articulating it. There are, moreover, in the *Metaphysics* and the *De Anima* a few tantalizing flashes of genius too brief to escape ambivalence. Yet if you know Aristotle's system well enough, you can, like a medieval thinker, move about in it and use it to think with, which is what I have been trying in our talks to do with the Hegelian system rather than merely expound it. I'm not sure, though, that I have succeeded in getting away enough from the detail.

. And Plato? What do you owe to direct contact with Plato?

. Compared with Aristotle, Plato is elusive and immature, but he is, notwithstanding, greater than his pupil. Indeed, he is to my mind the greatest of all philosophers. He brings his reader into the presence of spirit more surely than any other thinker. He commands this *amplior aether* because he is also a great artist, the only great artist among philosophers. He banished the poets from his ideal state partly through a theoretical error, partly from a touch of puritanism (almost his only fault), partly perhaps because he feared lest the poetry in him should interfere with his thinking. Nevertheless I learned from Plato rather than from Hegel that there is not reason without art. So of course I owe a vast deal to Plato. I am very sorry for any intelligent present-day British student who is introduced to philosophy through Locke instead of through the Greeks. It is like being born into a new world the wrong way up.

**AE.** Plato's severance of philosophy from poetry may, don't you think, have also been partly due to an excessive enthusiasm for Pythagoras and some exciting developments in mathematics, which were, perhaps, 'too newly born to be doubted'?

**E.** Possibly. One doesn't really know to what extent, after the great dialogues, mathematics got into his later metaphysical thinking. Mercifully Aristotle wasn't seduced.

**AE.** What about the social system of the *Republic*?

**E.** The first masterpiece of political theory is not a work to pass snap judgements on, but if you press me I will say this. The view that justice consists ideally in everybody doing his or her proper job and minding his or her proper business is sound enough. It never implied to Plato any tyrannical subjection of the citizen to the interests of the state, and today's reformers would do well to realize much more clearly than they do that not leisure but a worthwhile occupation which fits a man's or a woman's talents is the main ingredient in human happiness. On the other hand, I am not an egalitarian, but to sever genetically two classes of citizen was reactionary even in Plato's day. The sexual arrangements for the guardians don't attract me, but they may appeal one day to Women's Lib. enthusiasts. On the whole the *Republic* as political theory is more basic and central in its subject than anything since written, though one might have had to qualify that judgement if Aristotle's *Politics* had survived in a more complete shape.

**AE.** Wouldn't you also confess yourself indebted to Plato for lessons in gracious living and good manners? Wouldn't you love to have been Agathon's guest at the *Symposium*?

. Oh yes indeed. Was there ever a better party? Plato is about the only philosopher of the past whom I ever wished I could have met, except Spinoza. I said of Plato that he brings one more surely into the presence of spirit than any other thinker, and I would associate Spinoza with him in that regard. I think Hegel would have agreed, despite his sound criticism of Spinoza. I can well understand Samuel Alexander's remark that he would not object if his epitaph were *erravit cum Platone et Spinoza*. Both, moreover, were obviously very nice men. I don't really regret having been born sixty years after Hegel's death, and not for me the East German Kant. I would much rather have known my great-great-grandfather's dear friend David Hume, who lost his temper when my great-great-grandmother ticked him off for playing a hand at whist so badly.

. And the British idealists?

. I learned much from the formidable Bradley and the far suaver Bosanquet—from Bosanquet especially his treatment of individuality—but more and more they seemed to me to fall short beside Hegel. Joachim was different. He had reached his own position through the very profound study of Aristotle and Spinoza, and was much more Hegelian than the rest of the idealist school. But he shrank from trying to expound Hegel, familiar though he was with his writings. He told me that when he read Hegel some passages would strike him as brilliantly illuminating, others as totally obscure. When he read the same pages again, the alternation of light and darkness recurred, but the dark and light passages were no longer the same. I have had the same experience.

. Benedetto Croce?

. I was greatly attracted by the clarity of his mind and his consequently luminous style. Also by his wide scholarship in all fields of philosophy and literature. This impression of brilliance was confirmed when I was lucky enough to meet and talk with him in 1943. But I came to think later that philosophy must express itself in system more concrete than Croce's four 'distincts' present. I was fascinated, and still am, by Croce's theory of language, but I am not content to see philosophy exclude any dialectic of the forms of art. I think it was this bare lyricism in the aesthetic field which first made me realize that human philosophy cannot profitably ignore entirely the empirical, even if that must only enter philosophy in a partially sublated form. Nor could I follow Croce in denying to the physical even a minor share in the work of plastic art. I am also no longer convinced by Croce that the special sciences reveal nothing in the nature of things but their possible utility. It seems to me now, too, that Croce's rejection of transcendence leaves a humanism which does large justice to man's spirituality but isolates him from any universe beyond the *divenire* of human affairs.

**AE.** You don't think that something of that sort was inevitably the next creative stage of idealism after Hegel? If one rejects both theism and absolute spirit as closely connected myths but is nevertheless sure that man is spirit, doesn't Croce's system become pretty plausible? You decide that the four deepest 'distincts' in human experience are in the theoretical sphere intuition and concept, and in practice the useful or 'economic' and the moral. They are not opposites, but they develop with their own dialectic in and out of one another throughout human experience. On the other hand, all four break into pairs of opposites: beautiful and ugly, truth and error, useful and harmful, moral good and evil. So you can assign dialectic of opposites to everlasting *divenire*, the history of the human spirit, which is at once *res gestae* and *historia rerum gestarum*. You no longer need an unverifiable universe in which human history is alleged to be some sort of organic participant. Nature you dispose of as a purely economic construction.

**E.** It is a far better theory than the empiricisms and neo-scholasticisms which you just now invited me to embrace. It is civilized, not philistine, and very well worth study. One can think with it. But I do not find it does much to ease the 'burthen of the mystery'. It seems to leave man with nothing above him and nothing below him, weightless in outer space, as it were; whereas I see him determined from both directions. Man has the choice of self-transcendence or self-corruption always close at hand. To my mind his self-transcendence entails the immanence in him of what is beyond him, and it is the business of philosophy to show this as well as it can. But I begin to think that we have talked enough.

**E.** Do you think you have managed to say what you meant to say? One seldom does.

**E.** I have sometimes deliberately meandered because I was enjoying myself, but I think I have kept in view my main aims and expressed them with what clarity I could. I was trying to present a single hierarchical universe of spirit, which should overreach all Being and comprehend within itself all value, so that it might as such, as a universe, have a *raison d'être*. I wanted to show this notion as neither fantastic nor outmoded but compellingly sane. I wanted to show its bearing on the nature of individual men, and at the same time resist the encroachment of scientism in this field. I was, however, anxious that this hierarchy should not culminate in a particular self-subsistent perfect Being. I wanted neither the unconcerned God of Aristotle nor a deity conceived anthropomorphically and alleged to have created, and to be controlling, the world with a divine will which no theodicy can show to be devoid of caprice without postulating an unacceptable amount of pious ignorance. I fancy that man has a better right to existence than that allegedly conferred by a capricious act of creation for which he is told he ought to praise his maker.

**E.** Spiritual pride.

**E.** No; there is plenty to be said against the human species *sub specie temporis* on any account of its origin. I would not minimize the practical good which imaginative myth has done and can still do in controlling and inspiring human conduct, but only objective idealism seems to me to come anywhere near providing a *rational* ground for human intrinsic values, and Hegel, despite his appalling obscurity, is to me its most convincing advocate, not least by virtue of his unsurpassed philosophical pedigree. He, better than any other thinker, even than Aristotle, sums and justifies the aspirations of the human race. I have, on the other hand, only borrowed from Hegel, and discussed with you, what I wanted from him on a large scale. It would have been impossibly tedious in these talks to go into the detail of the dialectic, some of which I accept, some of which I question, some of which I reject, much of which I do not understand. Let me here also admit that what I have been endeavouring with

Hegel's help to say is not something new but something largely forgotten. At most I have been trying to express τὰ κοινὰ καινῶς, to put old wine from an undeservedly neglected cellar into new bottles. And not even all of it. I have certainly ignored much truth in Hegel which his disciples have praised, and many short-comings upon which his critics have fastened.

**AE.** Your hierarchy with no perfect self-subsistent Being at its summit, your absolute spirit which lives and has its being only in the struggle to overcome its self-alienation—isn't that another shape of anthropomorphism, a mere magnification of the human struggle? It reminds me of familiar sayings about human life like *Vivo ut vivam*, 'There's no failure but low aim', deserving success as more than commanding it, and so forth, sayings which suggest that the pursuit has its end entirely in itself.

**E.** Absolute spirit is both self-fulfilling and self-fulfilled; for the most part human life is only self-fulfilling. I said yesterday that human thought could do little more than *suggest* absolute spirit's moment of self-concentration. I meant to imply that its discursive moment is less intractable, that it is easier to show absolute spirit's self-fulfilling than its self-fulfilment. So there may well be in Hegel's conception of absolute spirit's activity, which I have attempted to share, a residue of anthropomorphism. At any rate I have honestly stressed the ignorance which overlaps human knowledge.

**AE.** I admit that you have least resembled Hegel when you have emphasized man's ignorance. But you have at the same time magnified, even perhaps rather paradoxically, the potential stature and scope of the human individual.

**E.** The fact is I am sick to death of the spectacle of humanity *en masse*. I don't doubt that at least from the beginning of this century, perhaps earlier, the human species has declined in quality in inverse proportion to its increase in quantity; declined in thought and action, art and morality, indeed by any standard you can think of except perhaps health and expectation of life. Leaving out black Africa, for which I have no figures, there are now more than three thousand million human beings alive, overpopulating this planet by at least 40 per cent. The majority of them are not significantly discriminable from one another and are, quite consistently, egalitarian in outlook so far as they have any outlook. The real danger with which the uncontrolled proliferation of mankind threatens us is not starvation. Science for some time will produce a sufficient quantity of food at the expense of its quality to balance Nature's continuing production of more and more inferior human beings. The danger is that, after a little token bloodshed and a great deal of dishonourable appeasement, man will lie flattened under the tyrannies which egalitarianism inevitably begets. The old like me, as they take us to the concentration camp, will cry with Cleopatra, 'The odds is gone,/ And there is nothing left remarkable/ Beneath the visiting moon'. That is why I shut my eyes and reflected on what an individual man can be and has been.

**E.** On that cheerful note I vanish, but I remind you again that the *Weltgeist* is not in a hurry.

# INDEX